STAAR
SUCCESS STRATEGIES

Grade 6
Reading

STAAR Test Review for the
State of Texas Assessments of Academic Readiness

Dear Future Exam Success Story:

Congratulations on your purchase of our study guide. Our goal in writing our study guide was to cover the content on the test, as well as provide insight into typical test taking mistakes and how to overcome them.

Standardized tests are a key component of being successful, which only increases the importance of doing well in the high-pressure high-stakes environment of test day. How well you do on this test will have a significant impact on your future- and we have the research and practical advice to help you execute on test day.

The product you're reading now is designed to exploit weaknesses in the test itself, and help you avoid the most common errors test takers frequently make.

How to use this study guide

We don't want to waste your time. Our study guide is fast-paced and fluff-free. We suggest going through it a number of times, as repetition is an important part of learning new information and concepts.

First, read through the study guide completely to get a feel for the content and organization. Read the general success strategies first, and then proceed to the content sections. Each tip has been carefully selected for its effectiveness.

Second, read through the study guide again, and take notes in the margins and highlight those sections where you may have a particular weakness.

Finally, bring the manual with you on test day and study it before the exam begins.

Your success is our success

We would be delighted to hear about your success. Send us an email and tell us your story. Thanks for your business and we wish you continued success-

Sincerely,

Mometrix Test Preparation Team

Need more help? Check out our flashcards at: http://MometrixFlashcards.com/STAAR

TABLE OF CONTENTS

Top 15 Test Taking Tips

1. Know the test directions, duration, topics, question types, how many questions
2. Setup a flexible study schedule at least 3-4 weeks before test day
3. Study during the time of day you are most alert, relaxed, and stress free
4. Maximize your learning style; visual learner use visual study aids, auditory learner use auditory study aids
5. Focus on your weakest knowledge base
6. Find a study partner to review with and help clarify questions
7. Practice, practice, practice
8. Get a good night's sleep; don't try to cram the night before the test
9. Eat a well balanced meal
10. Wear comfortable, loose fitting, layered clothing; prepare for it to be either cold or hot during the test
11. Eliminate the obviously wrong answer choices, then guess the first remaining choice
12. Pace yourself; don't rush, but keep working and move on if you get stuck
13. Maintain a positive attitude even if the test is going poorly
14. Keep your first answer unless you are positive it is wrong
15. Check your work, don't make a careless mistake

Reading Assessment

Root word and affix

A root word is the original word, before it is added onto. An affix is a prefix, infix, or suffix that is added onto a root word. Many affixes in the English language come from Latin or Greek origins. A prefix is added at the beginning of a root word, an infix, to the middle, and a suffix to the end of a root word. By looking at the meaning of a root word and the meaning of any affixes added to the root word, the reader can figure out the approximate meaning of the word. For example, the root word 'like' means to enjoy. The prefix 'dis-' means not. The reader can therefore say that the word 'dislike' means to not enjoy.

Example
Determine the meaning of the word 'prepay' by using knowledge of root words and affixes.

> A reader can use root words and affixes to figure out the general meaning of an unknown word. Knowing root words and affixes is helpful on tests where analogies are made using unfamiliar words. By figuring out the general meaning of an unknown word, a tester can figure out the general relationship between two words.

In the word 'prepay', the root word 'pay' means to give, such as to give money for goods or services. The prefix 'pre-' means before. The full word 'prepay' therefore means to give money before goods or services are granted. A person might prepay for a class, an appointment, or to reserve an item that has not arrived at the store yet.

Context clues

The term *context clues* refers to words or phrases found in the sentences surrounding an unknown. Context clues may include examples of the new word, synonyms, antonyms, definitions, or contrasting information. By using context clues in the surrounding sentences, the reader can determine approximately what the word means. A context clue in the form of an example may contain the words including 'such as', a dash, or a colon before stated information. A synonym is a word with a meaning similar to the unknown word, where an antonym is a word with a meaning opposite to the unknown word. A definition will state exactly what the new word means and contrasting information will include facts that are different from the new word.

Example 1
Read the following sentence and determine the meaning of the word 'pattering' based on context clues.

> "I like you! I like you!" she cried out, pattering down the walk; and she chirped and tried to whistle, which last she did not know how to do in the least. (From The Secret Garden by Frances Hodgson Burnett)

In the example sentence, the words 'down the walk' show that the character is moving on a sidewalk. The reader knows that the character is crying out and trying to chirp and whistle while moving, so the character cannot be completely out of breath. The character is also trying to reach the person or thing that she is crying out to. From these context clues, the reader can guess that the word 'pattering' means to walk quickly.

Example 2

Using context clues, determine the meaning of the word 'pestilent' in the following sentence.

> In fact, he declared it was of no use to work on his farm; it was the most pestilent little piece of ground in the whole country; everything about it went wrong, and would go wrong in spite of him. (From Rip Van Winkle by Washington Irving).

In the example, the word 'pestilent' is used to describe the ground. The character states that it was of no use to work on his farm and that everything about it went wrong. This indicates that the ground was difficult to work with, since the character had trouble with the ground no matter what he tried ('and would go wrong in spite of him'). The reader can assume, from these observations, that the word 'pestilent' means troublesome, annoying, or not allowing anything to grow, since this example is about the ground on a farm.

Denotative and connotative meanings

The denotative meaning of a word is the exact dictionary definition of the word. The connotative meaning of a word is the emotion conveyed by the use of the word in context. The word may have associated meaning in addition to its dictionary definition. For example, the word 'home' is defined in the dictionary as a place where a person or people live. When a reader sees the word in the following context: "Marisol walked briskly home, where the smell of fresh-baked apple pie wafted through the warm kitchen," the reader will associate the meaning of the word with coziness and a feeling of well-being. The connotative meaning of a word in a passage can be found by looking at the context clues.

Example

Determine the connotative meaning of the word 'ancient' in the following sentence.

> Amy pulled an *ancient* calculator out of the desk, and sat down to figure out how to use it.

In the example, the word 'ancient' literally means very old. The connotative meaning of the word ancient suggests that the calculator does not work as well as more modern versions. In technology, ancient is relative to what is currently being used. For example, a computer may be out of date in a couple years, whereas an ancient society may date back several thousand years.

Idioms

Idioms differ from the literal English meaning of words in the fact that they are expressions, or common ways of saying something. For example, 'to keep tabs on' is an idiomatic expression that is commonly used to communicate to someone to closely watch someone or something. Based on experience, determine the meaning of the idiom in the following sentence:

> Jared *hung his head* after viewing his score on the test and realizing that he had not studied the material long enough.

In the example, the phrase 'hung his head' is an idiom that means to look down with shame. By reading the rest of the sentence, the reader can see that the character did not study enough, which would lead him to be upset about his score on the test. Idioms can be figured out through the use of context clues, but are also learned through experience with the language.

Reference Materials

A print or digital dictionary can be used to find out many things about a word. A dictionary will show the correct pronunciation of a word, provide its meaning, and identify what part of speech the word is. It will also tell how the word was derived—that is, what words it came from originally. A dictionary will have a guide that shows how to sound out the words; it will use symbols to indicate sounds, and will also use sample sounds (the "a" in "bad," for instance). A dictionary lists all of the meanings of a word and the parts of speech the word can be used as.

A thesaurus is a reference book that gives synonyms of words. It is different from a dictionary because a thesaurus does not give definitions. A thesaurus can be helpful in finding the meaning of an unfamiliar word when reading. If the meaning of a synonym is known, then the meaning of the unfamiliar word will be known. Another time in which a thesaurus can be helpful is when writing. Using a thesaurus helps authors to vary their word choice.

A glossary is a list of terms and their definitions that can be found at the back of certain types of books, such as textbooks or reference books. A glossary does not have the definitions of all words, like a dictionary, but instead gives the definitions of the important terms within that particular book which are either uncommon or newly introduced. One may use a glossary when reading a book about economics or a chapter in a science textbook, for example, to define some of the technical terms within the text.

Historical and Cultural Setting

Historical context influences literature in a number of ways. The style of the author's writing can be impacted by the historical period during which it was written (e.g., Dickens wrote at a time when authors were paid by the word; this is why his novels are so long). Obviously, the setting of the book includes its historical context. In addition, dialect may be a function of the historical period of the book. When a reader understands the historical context of a particular book, he or she can have a deeper understanding of the novel. Knowing about the time period in which the author wrote, as well as the time period discussed in the novel, helps the reader understand some of the author's choices, including character motivations.

<u>Example</u>
Slavery used to be the norm in Southern states. One of the major ways in which the historical context of slavery impacted literature coming out of the South was the birth of the slave narrative. Slaves wanted to have their experiences documented. After the Civil War, former slaves wrote their stories. These slave narratives have given historians valuable firsthand accounts of life in the South. From a literary perspective, slave narratives are one of the most important genres of African-American writing. Slavery influenced literature by

delving into themes of power, racial injustice, and equality. Literature from this time period can help the reader better understand the perspectives and experiences of the slaves themselves, as well as the slave holders.

Memoirs and personal narratives

A memoir is a form of literature where the author tells about only a specific part of his life. Memoirs do not tell the author's story from birth to old age. They are often written by people in politics or in business, and tell about the author's career and successes. A memoir written by a person would include many intimate details about the person's feelings that a biographer might only guess at. The format would be much more personal than the format of a biography as well. The word memoir is French for "memory" and that is what a memoir is—the memories of an individual about his or her life.

A personal narrative is most often the first type of writing a person will do. In a personal narrative the author tells a story about his life. It can contain as much detail, dialogue, and excitement as the author wants to put into it. Personal narratives are often more entertaining because they are very personal.

Both memoirs and personal narratives are types of autobiographical works. They are written about the author to tell others about the author's life and experiences. The main difference is that autobiographies focus on the whole of the author's life, instead of focusing only on small parts of it.

Authors Purpose

The author's purpose is going to be their reason for writing the paper or story. Some authors may write with the purpose of entertainment in mind. Most fiction novels would fall under this category. The author may also write with the purpose of trying to persuade or convince the reader. A Proposition and Support paper would be an example of this, where an author gives their opinion and then tries to convince the reader to see something from their point of view. An author can also write with the purpose of informing or teaching the reader. As the reader reads a paper they should always try to figure out the author's purpose for writing as this will help them to better understand the message that the author is trying to convey.

Text structure

Cause and effect
The term *cause and effect* means when one event happens in a text, another event occurs because of it. The term *chronology* refers to the order of events over time. For example, a text may discuss the school policy that, when a student is late to school too many times, they receive a detention. The student being late too many times is the cause and the detention is the effect. Chronology of events in a story can occur over a short, or extended, period of time. For example, if a text discusses the rise of the Roman Empire, it may include the rulers of the Roman Empire over time and any changes that occurred during each ruler's time in power.

<u>Compare and Contrast</u>

Comparison and contrast involves showing similarities and differences between items or events. As an example the author may write about a Compare and Contrast about cats and dogs. They can start by giving a brief description of the two. Then they will want to point out all of the similarities, such as; they both have tails, and both are kept as pets. Next they will explain the differences, such as; dogs are canines, while cats are felines. They will try to provide as much detail as possible about both the similarities and the differences.

Theme

The theme of a passage is what the reader learns from the text or the passage. It is the lesson or moral contained in the passage. It also is a unifying idea that is used throughout the text; it can take the form of a common setting, idea, symbol, design, or recurring event. A passage can have two or more themes that convey its overall idea. The theme or themes of a passage are often based on universal themes. They can frequently be expressed using well-known sayings about life, society, or human nature, such as "Hard work pays off" or "Good triumphs over evil." Themes are not usually stated explicitly. The reader must figure them out by carefully reading the passage. Themes are often the reason why passages are written; they give a passage unity and meaning. Themes are created through plot development. The events of a story help shape the themes of a passage.

Explain why "Take care of what you care about" accurately describes the theme of the following excerpt.

> Luca collected baseball cards. But, Luca wasn't very careful with them. He left them around the house. His dog liked to chew. Luca and his friend Bart were looking at his collection. Then, they went outside. When Luca got home, he saw his dog chewing on his cards. They were ruined.

This excerpt tells the story of a boy who is careless with his baseball cards and leaves them lying around. His dog ends up chewing them and ruining them. The lesson is that if you care about something, you need to take care of it. This is the point of the story. The theme is the lesson that a story teaches. Some stories have more than one theme, but this is not really true of this excerpt. The reader needs to figure out the theme based on what happens in the story. Sometimes, as in the case of fables, the theme is stated directly in the text. However, this is not usually the case.

Rule of three and the magic helper

The rule of three is based on the assumption that things that come in threes are more entertaining, funnier, and more effective than any other number. Research shows that the reader can better absorb ideas within the literature if they are grouped into threes. For example, many stories group characters into groups of three. There are stories about the three little pigs, Goldilocks and the three bears, and the three blind mice. Authors will also often use the number three within the story where a character has to complete three tasks or complete an action three times.

The magic helper is an element often used when the main character must accomplish a daunting or even an impossible task. The main character may receive aid from a fairy godmother, a genie, or just a person with a special skill or power, who makes the previously difficult or impossible task doable. The helper is usually with the character during all the challenges in the story.

Poetry and Figurative Language

Poetry is meant to be read aloud, or recited, and listened to. Poets use rhythm to give their poems a melody or cadence. Rhythm is the stress and flow of words in a poem. Certain words and syllables are meant to be read with more emphasis than others. Poets use stressed and unstressed syllables of words to give their poems a melodic sound. One way poets develop rhythm is by the repetition of certain words. In the given example, Walt Whitman uses repetition of the word "sound" to develop the rhythm of the piece.

<u>Rhythm example</u>
The following excerpt is from the poem, "Song of Myself" by Walt Whitman:

> I hear the sound I love, the sound of the human voice;
> I hear all sounds running together, combined, fused or following;
>
> Sounds of the city, and sounds out of the city—sounds of the day and night;
> Talkative young ones to those that like them—the loud laugh of work-people
> at their meals;

Figurative language refers to a number of ways writers deviate from literal meaning in text. Some common forms of figurative language include metaphor, simile, hyperbole, irony, and personification.

A simile is a comparison made using the words *like* or *as*. An example of a simile is: She was as fast as lightning as she ran down the track. The author is comparing the runner with lightning using the word *as*.

A metaphor is a comparison of two unlike things. A metaphor is different from a simile because it does not use the words *like* or *as*. An example of a metaphor is: She was lighting running down the track. The author is comparing the runner with lightning but does not use the words *like* or *as*.

Personification is a figure of speech in which an object is given human qualities. An example of personification is: The teapot hummed when the water was boiling. Humming is something that humans do, but here it is attributed to the teapot.

<u>Simile example</u>
Read the following excerpt from "The Raven" by Edgar Allan Poe, identify a simile, and explain what it means:

> Till I scarcely more than muttered "Other friends have flown before—
> On the morrow he [the raven] will leave me, as my hopes have flown before."
> Then the bird said, "Nevermore."

The one simile in the excerpt from "The Raven" by Edgar Allan Poe is: "On the morrow he [the raven] will leave me, *as* my hopes have flown before."

The simile compares the raven's departure with the departure of the narrator's hopes. The narrator is no longer hopeful; his hopes have flown away from him in much the same way that a bird flies away. Thus, the raven's flying is compared to the departure of the narrator's hopes.

<u>Metaphor example</u>
Read the following excerpt from "The Raven" by Edgar Allan Poe, identify the metaphor, and discuss how it impacts the text:

> And the raven, never flitting, still is sitting, still is sitting
> On the pallid bust of Pallas just above my chamber door;
> And his eyes have all the seeming of a demon's that is dreaming

One metaphor in the excerpt from "The Raven" by Edgar Allan Poe is: "And his eyes have all the seeming of a demon's that is dreaming"
The metaphor compares the raven's eyes with that of a demon, thereby, comparing the bird to a demon. This indicates that the speaker thinks there is evil in the bird. The metaphor helps contribute to the overall tone of the poem and the reader's understanding of how the speaker views the bird.

Plot

All plots begin with a setting, where the story takes place. In some stories the plot is more obvious than in others. Setting plays a key role in the progression of events in some stories and is less intertwined in the plot of other stories. In order for a plot to develop, it must include characters, which can be human or another type of entity. A plot will start at one point, either before a conflict occurs, after a conflict occurs, or in the middle of a conflict. The plot will continue to develop by the introduction of new ideas and events centered on the main conflict in the story. The action in the story will rise until a climax is reached within the conflict. The climax can also be referred to as the turning point in the story, since the climax is where a decision is made and the action starts to wind down; this is called the denouement. The conflict is usually resolved in some way by the end of the story. Some conflicts are left open-ended, so that the reader is left to decide what really happened at the end of the story.

<u>Example</u>
Read the following plot and analyze what event is missing from the plot sequence.

> Martin's family decided to go camping at the local park over the weekend.
> They packed all the camping necessities and drove to the park. Thick sheets
> of rain poured down all day, so that they were stuck in their tent.

Martin and his family forgot to check the weather forecast before they left for their camping trip. To fill in the missing detail, the author may write: "Martin and his family checked the forecast and saw that it was going to rain, but decided to go camping anyway." The flow of the story is broken up by the sudden realization that it is raining, something that could be prevented by adding in the missing detail.

When details are missing from a plot sequence, the audience has trouble following the action in a story. By adding in additional details, the point of each step in a story can be made clearer to the audience.

Main conflict

Example 1
Read the following sentence from The Call of the Wild by Jack London and describe the main conflict in the sentence. Explain how the conflict may be resolved.

> The breaking down of discipline likewise affected the dogs in their relations with one another.

Based on the information in the sentence, an event has caused the dogs, the characters in the story, to not follow their regular routine. The sentence indicates that there has been a breaking down of discipline which is affecting how the dogs relate to each other. In order to solve this conflict, discipline needs to be restored. However, in order to return to previous relations between the dogs, any problems that are in the way of conflict resolution need to be taken care of. The word likewise means also, which tells the reader that other avenues are being affected in the story besides the relations between the dogs.

Example 2
Read the following sentence and explain the main conflict between the two characters:

> Joe stared angrily at Jamie's retreating back as Jamie raced away down the field with Joe's soccer ball.

The main conflict in the sentence is that Jamie has Joe's soccer ball. There may be additional conflicts between the two characters, but none are evident from the evidence shown in the sentence. In any story, a conflict may be minor and only affect part of the story, or be the main focus, taking an entire story to solve a conflict between characters. In the context of the sentence, it is not clear whether or not the entire story will revolve around Jamie taking Joe's soccer ball. However, the current conflict is based upon that information in the sentence.

Problem resolution

The term *problem resolution* usually indicates the result of a conflict in a story. Conflict between characters, within a character, or against an external element is necessary in order to have a plot for a story. Without conflict, no events would occur to form the story. A conflict will come to a climax, and then conclude in some way. The resolution of a problem may be open-ended, end tragically, or end in a way that is beneficial for all parties involved. The *problem resolution* typically occurs near the end of a story, after the climax and conclusion have occurred. A problem may be resolved by the characters involved within the conflict or by an external event; an upcoming resolution may be foreshadowed in the text, or may be completely unexpected by the reader. If the *problem resolution* is completely unexpected, it is a *twist* in the story.

Dialect and Conversational Voice

Dialect is any distinct variety of a language, especially one spoken in a region or part of a. country. When an author uses dialect it helps give the reader a better understanding of the character and their background, education, and culture. This can be important for the author of a story with a large cast. They can give each character their own unique voice and identity through the use of dialect. Another way for the author to form a quick relationship between the narrator and the reader is by the use of conversational voice. This gives the reader the impression that the character is speaking directly to them or to another character in a casual manner, instead of a more formal voice

Character trait

The traits of a character may include how they act and physical characteristics, that are unique to a specific character. For example, a character may be outgoing, which means he or she likes to talk a lot, or have bright red hair. These are both character traits.
An author uses character traits to describe a character in a story. Character traits help the reader to learn more about how the character acts and what they look like. By comparing the different character traits in a story, the reader can see similarities and differences between characters. The author includes character traits to help the reader understand why a character may act a certain way in the story. For example, a character who is shy may not want to talk with a lot of people in a new classroom, but a character who is outgoing may want to talk with many.

Example
Read the following sentence from *How the Whale Got His Throat*. State the character traits that the reader learns from the sentence.

> "He ate the starfish and the garfish, and the crab and the dab, and the plaice and the dace, and the skate and his mate, and the mackereel and the pickereel, and the really truly twirly-whirly eel."

In this example, the reader finds out that the character likes to eat seafood a great deal. Since the title includes the word "whale" and by applying previous knowledge about what whales eat, the reader can assume that a whale is being described in the sentence, as it is eating all kinds of seafood as described above. The reader can also assume, from the variety described, that the whale it not picky about what type of seafood it eats.

Points of view

The point of view of a text is the perspective from which it is told. Every literary text has a narrator or person who tells the story. The two main points of view that authors use are first person and third person. If a narrator is also the main character, or protagonist, the text is written in first-person point of view. The author writes with the word I. Third-person point of view is probably the most common point of view that authors use. Using third person, authors refer to each character using the words he or she. In third-person omniscient, the narrator is not a character in the story and tells the story of all of the characters at the same time.

<u>Limitations of first person</u>
First person point of view is told from the perspective of only one person. Since this is the case, the reader only gets one side of the story, without any other angles on what may have happened in the text, such as in a personal narrative. For example, the book *The Catcher in the Rye* is told from a first person point of view, that of Holden Caulfield. Alternately, the third person point of view gives a more objective, or whole, view of a story as it is viewed and told from many different perspectives. With this, the reader often knows what is going on in the mind of each character in the story.

Style, tone, and mood

An author can vary the feel of a text by changing the style, tone, and mood of each sentence. The style of a text refers to whether the author uses long, flowing sentences, short, choppy sentences, or something in-between. The text may be organized in short lines, short paragraphs, or long paragraphs. The tone of a paper helps to establish the mood of the text. Tone involves the attitude that the author displays in the paper. For example, the author may feel exuberant about a sunny day, but feel down on a gloomy day. The words that the author uses to describe the scene and situation in the story help to define its tone. The mood of a story may be uplifting, down, scared, or excited, again, depending upon the words the author uses. All of these elements: style, tone, and mood, can affect how the reader feels about the story.

<u>Example 1</u>
Describe the tone of the following sentence from "The Adventure of the Speckled Band" by Sir Arthur Conan Doyle:

> Then creeping up to me and making a trumpet of his hand, he whispered into my ear again so gently that it was all that I could do to distinguish the words.

The tone of the sentence is mysterious. The words "creeping" and "whispered into my ear" make the reader wonder why the character needs to be quiet in the story. The characters in the sentence seem to be waiting for something to happen, making the reader may feel that they need to hold their breath while waiting to see what happens to the characters in the story. The tone of the sentence is appropriately mysterious, since the story is written as a mystery. By creating suspense in the text, the author makes the reader want to see what happens next.

<u>Example 2</u>
Describe the style and mood of the following sentence from The Adventures of Tom Sawyer by Mark Twain:

> He surveyed the fence, and all gladness left him and a deep melancholy settled down upon his spirit.

The style of the sentence is fully descriptive of the character's feelings, painting a picture in the reader's mind of the character's thoughts. The author uses the word 'and' twice to signify the sinking spirits of the character in the sentence. The mood of the sentence mirrors the emotion of the character, as the character goes from level-headed to quite sad, from which the reader can deduce that the character does not want to do something, which has brought down his mood as a result. In this particular scenario, the character does not want to spend a long time whitewashing a fence while he had other plans on such a beautiful day. The style of the sentence is direct; it explains how the character feels in the story.

Media Literacy

Media literacy involves being able to analyze, evaluate, and create messages in a wide variety of media forms. There are many forms of media including television, internet, printed materials, like books and newspapers, and radios. Since each of these will convey messages differently it is important to be able to comprehend and analyze these messages.

Television and printed media

Television is one of many media used to affect a person's emotions, and also behavior. Different images, words, graphics, and sounds can be used to create meaning. For example, advertisements directed at children will often show other kids having fun doing an activity. The bright colors and obvious excitement on their faces will entice a child watching the advertisement to want the item. The child sees other kids having fun, and wants to have fun too. Adults can be influenced by media in much the same way.

Journalists will write positive stories about a person or product that encourages the adult to want to try a product or back a certain person because of the results they read about. Images can also be used to appeal to a person's emotions. A sad image such as a neglected animal or a starving child will often result in compassion from the viewer and can even spur the viewer to some action, such as donating money to a cause.

Drawing Conclusions

An inference is a conclusion or generalization that the reader makes based on the information provided within a text. Certain facts are included to help a reader come to a specific conclusion. For example, a story may open with a man trudging through the snow on a cold winter day, dragging a sled behind him. The reader can logically infer from the setting of the story that the man is wearing heavy winter clothes in order to stay warm. Information is implied based on the setting of a story, which is why setting is an important element of the text. If the same man in the example was trudging down a beach on a hot summer day, dragging a surf board behind him, the reader would assume that the man is not wearing heavy clothes. The reader makes inferences based on their own experiences and the information presented to them in the story.

Example 1
Read the following sentence and draw a conclusion based upon the information presented:

> "You know the reason Mother proposed not having any presents this Christmas was because it is going to be a hard winter for everyone; and she thinks we ought not to spend money for pleasure, when our men are suffering so in the army." (from *Little Women* by Louisa May Alcott, p. 3)

Based on the information in the sentence, the reader can conclude, or infer, that the men are away at war while the women are still at home. The pronoun 'our' gives a clue to the reader that the character is speaking about men she knows. In addition, the reader can assume that the character is speaking to a brother or sister, since the term Mother is used by the character while speaking to another person. The reader can also come to the conclusion that the characters celebrate Christmas, since it is mentioned in the context of the sentence. In the sentence, the Mother is presented as an unselfish character who is opinionated and thinks about the well-being of other people.

Paraphrasing and summarizing

Paraphrasing and summarizing are two methods one can use to help them understand what they read. When paraphrasing, one puts what they have read into their own words, rephrasing what the author has written to make it their own, to "translate" all of what the author says to their own words, including as many details as they can. When summarizing, on the other hand, one does not include many details, but rather simply the main idea of the text. Often times, a summary can be done in just one sentence, boiling down the author's words into just main idea.

Example summary
Read the following paragraph and then give a one sentence summary statement:

> People used to know their bankers. Now, many people do their banking online. With a login and password, customers can have access to their accounts with up to the minute information. Users can keep track of their spending, transfer money between accounts, and pay bills online, all from the comfort of home.

In order to summarize, one has to identify the main idea and any supporting ideas in the author's work. The summary is an overview of the author's paragraph and will tell what it is about without getting into any of the details. The summary needs to be broad enough to cover all of the information in the author's paragraph. Here is a possible summary statement for the above paragraph:
Most people nowadays find it convenient to do their banking online instead of at a branch office.

Example paraphrasing
Read the following sentences and then paraphrase the material:

> The government is debating a new health care system for our country. The Senate and the House of Representatives have both passed bills; now they need to resolve these two bills into one bill that a majority can agree on.

When paraphrasing information, one needs to read carefully and pay attention to details, then put the material away and write or tell it in their own words. One does not want to look at the material while paraphrasing to avoid plagiarizing by accident. Here is one example of a way to paraphrase the sentences:
Our government is trying to adopt a new health care system. The Senate has passed a bill and so has the House of Representatives. Their bills are different so now they have to compromise on one bill that can be passed.

Text evidence

The term *text evidence* refers to information included in a text that supports the main point of the paper. A reader can draw conclusions or generalizations based upon information found in a text, in which the author will deliberately include key points that serve as supporting details for the main point. For example, the main point of a paper may state: The average yearly rainfall in the city has risen by 2 inches per year since 1999. The paper would go on to include the amount of rainfall for each month or season and any contributing factors that may be causing an increase in yearly rainfall. Additional facts, or text evidence to support the point that yearly rainfall is rising in the city would help to prove that the author's main point is correct.

Example 1
Draw a conclusion based on the following sentence from The Adventures of Tom Sawyer by Mark Twain:

> He had discovered a great law of human action, without knowing it—
> namely, that in order to make a man or a boy covet a thing, it is only
> necessary to make the thing difficult to attain.

The reader can conclude from the sentence that the character did not set out to learn something, but through an action, the character learned that people will want what is hard to attain. The character learned a fact about human nature; that a person will value something more if they have to work hard for it than if it is simply given to them. The word *covet* means to desire, which the character learns can be manipulated by making an item or an outcome more difficult to grasp. In everyday life, this could apply toward taking a hard test and doing well. If someone studies for a hard test and does well, the person will value their score more than if the test was very easy and he or she did not study for the test.

Main idea and supporting details

The main idea in a passage is usually located in the first paragraph or two of text. Having the main idea near the beginning of the passage allows the author to grab the reader's attention and let him or her know what the rest of the passage will discuss. To find the main idea in a passage, the read should ask questions while reading, such as "What is this passage about? What does the author want the reader to know about the topic?" The supporting details will provide evidence that the main idea is correct. Supporting details are found in the body of a passage. The supporting details often provide examples of the main idea. For example, a passage may contain the main idea: "Ellis Island was an entry-point to America for many immigrants during the Industrial Revolution." A supporting detail for this main idea may be "Immigrants were examined for contagious diseases at Ellis Island before being granted entry to America."

Example 1
Read the excerpt below. Identify and discuss the main idea.

> Students who have jobs while attending high school tend not to have as much time to
> complete their homework as other students. They also do not have time for other
> activities. We should try to persuade our young people to concentrate on doing well in

school, not to concentrate on making money. Having a job while you are a student is harmful.

The main idea of the excerpt is actually the last sentence: "Having a job while you are a student is harmful." This is what the excerpt is mostly about. The other sentences contain supporting information: students who have jobs don't have as much time for homework; students with jobs don't have time for as many activities. These are both supporting details that tell more about the main idea. The third sentence deals with a persuasive argument; it is another kind of detail. Only the last sentence tells what the excerpt is mostly about. Main ideas are sometimes found in a topic sentence at the start of a text or in the concluding sentence, which is the case in this excerpt.

Conclusion

The conclusion of a text is typically found in the last one or two paragraphs of the text. A conclusion wraps-up the text and reminds the reader of the main point of the text. The conclusion is the author's way of leaving the reader with a final note to remember about the paper and comes after all the supporting points of the text have been presented. For example, a paper about the importance of avoiding too much sunlight may have a conclusion that reads: By limiting sun exposure to 15 minutes a day and wearing sunscreen of at least SPF 15, a person can reduce their risk of getting skin cancer later in life.

Construction of an Argument

When reading a persuasive text, the first thing a reader should do is follow the way in which the author is building the argument. Look for the main contention that the author has and also the ways in which the author adds to their argument. Usually the author will include supporting information to their claims, but that supporting information needs to be valid in order to support the claim. Look at the supporting evidence and notice where it comes from. Ask yourself if the evidence is based on facts and if the facts come from a reliable source or from a source that cannot be researched and confirmed. Be cautious of emotional claims that are based more on feelings than on fact. Throw out any claims that lack proper verification.

When discussing a controversial subject, an author has a duty to bring up both sides of an argument. The author may feel a certain way, but should still include opposing viewpoints in order to have a seemingly objective passage or essay. An author can, of course, refute the viewpoints but would need to use logical reasons why and cite any evidence that she wishes to include as testimony. In some cases, the author may not wish to side with either position, but merely to address the issues and give conflicting evidence so that the reader can form his own opinion about an issue.

Fact and opinion

When deciding whether information is fact or opinion, a reader needs to look at whether or not the information is well-accepted by experts, in addition to being backed-up by outside sources. A fact is something that is true, regardless of what the author thinks, on the contrary, an opinion is what the author thinks, without regard to evidence to back-up that claim. For example, for a paper about caves, a fact may read: Extensive cave systems run through the soft limestone of Central Texas. An opinion may read: Caving, also called spelunking, is an enjoyable recreational activity. It is a fact that caves run throughout Central Texas, but it is the author's opinion that spelunking is an enjoyable recreational activity.

Example
Decide whether the following sentence is a fact or opinion. Explain your reasoning.

> The new school year will start one week before Labor Day and end on May 31st.

This sentence is a fact. The school calendar is set each year to start and finish on a certain day and while days are built into the schedule to account for bad weather, right now, the school year is set to end on May 31st. The information is factual because it is established by the school district. An opinion would express a personal feeling about the situation. For example, in the sentence, an opinion might state: The new school year should start after Labor Day and end the second week in June, so that students have the full month of August for summer.

Organizational Patterns

When writing there are a variety of ways that an author can choose to organize their story. It is important for them to choose the pattern that best presents their information, as not all patterns will work for every piece of writing. For example, if an author wants to write a story about a series of events that happened one week they would organize their story in Chronological Order. However, if they were writing an informational text an author may want to use Order of Importance to organize the paper. Order of Importance would present their information from the most important point to the least important one.

Problem and Solution
Problem and Solution is an organizational pattern where the author will present some information as a problem and will then discuss a solution or attempted solution. In Problem and Solution there is generally one main problem, but that one problem may have several possible solutions. For example, let's say that Billy wants a new video game but does not have the money. There are several possible solutions to this. First he could just try asking his mom to buy it for him. If that does not work he could get a job mowing grass until he has enough money to buy it. A third solution would be if he is really patient he could wait until his birthday and ask for it then. Problem and Solution can sometimes be confused with Cause and Effect. However, the easy way to tell them apart is in Cause and Effect there is a cause or problem and then it discusses the effects but does not give a solution.

Proposition and Support
In Proposition and Support an author will state a proposition that is their opinion that they will debate in the paper. The topic is generally something that readers will feel uncertain about and may not already have an opinion on. The author will then give support for his argument. The support should include facts, statistics, logic and reasoning. The more hard evidence an author can give the reader the better it will help convince them to see things from the author's point of view.

- 16 -

Faulty Reasoning

A logical fallacy occurs when an author attempts to use common errors in reasoning to persuade his readers. Two types of logical fallacies are "slippery slope" and "hasty generalizations." In a "slippery slope" fallacy, the author asserts a certain effect is certain when a specific cause exists, even though this may not be true. (For example, "If you study hard, you will ace the test.") "Hasty generalization" fallacies draw a conclusion too early without finishing analyzing the details of the argument. Writers of persuasive texts often use these techniques because they are very effective. In order to identify logical fallacies, readers need to read carefully and ask questions as they read. Thinking critically means not taking everything at face value. Readers need to critically evaluate an author's argument to make sure that the logic used is sound.

Authors will sometimes appeal to the reader's emotion in an attempt to persuade or to distract the reader from the weakness of his argument. For instance, the author may try to inspire the pity of the reader by delivering a heart-rending story. An author also might use the bandwagon approach, in which he suggests that his opinion is correct because it is held by a majority of people. Some authors resort delivering insults and harsh words against an opponent in an attempt to distract. In advertising, a common appeal is the testimonial, in which a famous person endorses a product. Of course, the fact that a celebrity likes something should not really mean anything to the reader. These and other emotional appeals are usually evidence of poor reasoning and a weak argument.

Interpreting Graphical Information

A line graph is typically used for measuring trends over time. It is set up along a vertical and a horizontal axis. The variables being measured are listed along the left side and the bottom side of the axes. Points are then plotted along the graph, such that they correspond with their values for each variable. For instance, imagine a line graph measuring a person's income for each month of the year. If the person earned $1500 in January, there would be a point directly above January, perpendicular to the horizontal axis, and directly to the right of $1500, perpendicular to the vertical axis. Once all of the lines are plotted, they are connected with a line from left to right. This line provides a nice visual illustration of the general trends. For instance, using the earlier example, if the line sloped up, it would be clear that the person's income had increased over the course of the year.

The bar graph is one of the most common visual representations of information. Bar graphs are used to illustrate sets of numerical data. The graph has a vertical axis, along which numbers are listed, and a horizontal axis, along which categories, words, or some other indicators are placed. One example of a bar graph is a depiction of the respective heights of famous basketball players: the vertical axis would contain numbers ranging from five to eight feet, and the horizontal axis would contain the names of the players. The length of the bar above the player's name would illustrate his height, as the top of the bar would stop perpendicular to the height listed along the left side. In this representation, then, it would be easy to see that Yao Ming is taller than Michael Jordan, because Yao's bar would be higher.

A pie chart, also known as a circle graph, is useful for depicting how a single unit or category is divided. The standard pie chart is a circle within which wedges have been cut and labeled. Each of these wedges is proportional in size to its part of the whole. For instance, consider a pie chart representing a student's budget. If the student spends half her money on rent, then the pie chart will represent that amount with a line through the center of the pie. If she spends a quarter of her money on food, there will be a line extending from the edge of the circle to the center at a right angle to the line depicting rent. This illustration would make it clear that the student spends twice as much money on rent as she does on food. The pie chart is only appropriate for showing how a whole is divided.

Practice Test #1

Practice Questions

Questions 1 – 12 pertain to the following short story:

A World of White: The Iditarod Trail

(1) Imagine clinging desperately to your sled as brutal winds batter your body. The path ahead appears and disappears like a mirage, frequently obscured by blowing curtains of snow. You are freezing and sweating at the same time. Your throat burns with thirst, and your body aches with fatigue. You know your dogs must feel it too, so you encourage them to press on to the next checkpoint. All around you, the world is endless, empty, and white. Welcome to the Iditarod Trail.

(2) Alaska's Iditarod Trail is the world's most famous sled dog racing venue. But the trail is older than the sport of sled dog racing. In fact, the Iditarod Trail was first established in the early 1900s, during the Alaskan gold rush. In those days, dog teams were used for work, hauling thousands of pounds of gold from landlocked Iditarod to the port of Anchorage. But in faraway Nome, also known for gold, six-year-old George Allen had the idea to put together a race to see whose sled dogs were fastest, and the sport of sled dog racing was born.

(3) Though the Iditarod Trail race is the most famous race in the sport of sled dog racing, the first race along the trail was actually a race to save lives. In 1925, a diphtheria outbreak began in Nome. To prevent an epidemic that could kill thousands, doctors were desperate for the vaccine serum, but the closest serum was in Anchorage. The train ran from Anchorage to the village of Nenana, but that was still 674 miles from Nome. A cry for help was sent by the doctors, and in the midst of the blizzards and windstorms of January, the call was answered. Twenty brave mushers drove their dogs in a frantic relay, carrying 300,000 bottles of serum from Nenana to Nome. They followed the Iditarod Trail.

(4) Dog sledding, or "mushing," became quite popular after that heroic journey, but by the 1960s, it had lost popularity and the Iditarod Trail had been largely forgotten. There were a few lovers of mushing, however, who worked tirelessly to reestablish the Iditarod Trail and create a new sled dog race that used the trail as its course. The first official race was held in 1967 to celebrate the centennial of the purchase of Alaska from Russia. The race involved 58 drivers who mushed 56 miles in two days. This race was a success, but the popularity and future of the Iditarod Trail was still in question.

(5) In March of 1973, the first Anchorage to Nome Iditarod Trail race was organized and held. This race was much longer than previous races, covering more than 1,000 miles—the whole Iditarod Trail. Thirty-four mushers began the race, but only 22 were able to finish. After the 1973 race, the popularity of the Iditarod Trail finally grew and was firmly established. In 1978, the Iditarod Trail became a National Historic Trail.

- 19 -

(6) The modern Iditarod Trail race is open to mushers over 18 years old who have qualified in a recognized race of 200 miles or more. For younger mushers between 14 and 18 years old, the Junior Iditarod offers a 130-mile version of the race. Many Junior Iditarod participants go on to compete in the Iditarod Trail race, as the Junior Iditarod is good practice for the grueling trek of the main race. All mushers must prepare for the race extensively, often for months before the race. Many mushers run their dogs more than 1,500 miles in preparation, giving them experience in all types of weather and terrain.

(7) To enter the Iditarod Trail race, participants must pay an entrance fee. Then they must travel to Anchorage with their dogs. In Anchorage, they attend a mushers' banquet where they are given their racing order numbers. Afterwards, all participating dogs are checked by a veterinarian and marked by race officials to prevent dog switching mid-race, which is not allowed. The dogs are even drug tested at the beginning and at checkpoints throughout the race to prevent cheating! Finally, the sleds and equipment are checked. Then participants are ready to start the race.

(8) On the morning of the Iditarod Trail race, mushers leave Anchorage in their assigned racing order. They are sent out one at a time, at two-minute intervals. For more than a week—sometimes up to three weeks—they travel throughout Alaska, stopping at designated checkpoints all along the Iditarod Trail as they make their way to Nome. When all participants have reached Nome, another mushers' banquet is held. Awards are given, and everyone is applauded for their achievement. Win or lose, the mushers know that only the toughest of the tough have what it takes to finish the race and conquer the great Iditarod Trail.

1. What does the simile in paragraph 1 describe?

Ⓐ The snow

Ⓑ The path

Ⓒ The musher's throat

Ⓓ The dogs

2. What does "landlocked" mean in paragraph 2?

Ⓐ Barricaded by hills

Ⓑ Built underground

Ⓒ Not on a waterway

Ⓓ In the mountains

3. What two cities are on the ends of the Iditarod Trail?

Ⓐ Anchorage and Nome

Ⓑ Nome and Nenana

Ⓒ Iditarod and Anchorage

Ⓓ Nenana and Iditarod

4. What is the author's main purpose in writing this article?

Ⓐ To encourage mushers to race on the Iditarod Trail

Ⓑ To inform the reader about the 1925 diphtheria outbreak

Ⓒ To describe the terrain of Alaska

Ⓓ To educate the reader about the Iditarod Trail

5. In paragraph 3, which words best convey the feelings of the doctors in Nome in 1925?

Ⓐ "Epidemic" and "diphtheria"

Ⓑ "Blizzards" and "windstorms"

Ⓒ "Brave" and "frantic relay"

Ⓓ "Desperate" and "cry for help"

6. Why did the author choose to write this article in third-person point of view?

Ⓐ Historical overviews are best written in third person

Ⓑ The author has never been to Alaska

Ⓒ Third person is the required point of view in nonfiction writing

Ⓓ This article is not written in third-person point of view

7. In what year did the Iditarod Trail become a National Historic Trail?

Ⓐ 1967

Ⓑ 1973

Ⓒ 1978

Ⓓ 1981

8. Which of the following is the best summary of the history of the Iditarod Trail race?

Ⓐ After the Iditarod Trail became a National Historic Trail, the race became more popular, and today many mushers participate each year

Ⓑ After a slow start in 1967, the Iditarod Trail race became firmly established in 1973, and it continues in popularity today

Ⓒ In the first race in 1973, 34 mushers began the race, but only 22 were able to finish, proving that the race was just too hard

Ⓓ Mushers between 14 and 18 years of age can race in the Junior Iditarod, while those over 18 can participate in the main race if they qualify

9. How is this article organized?

Ⓐ Chronologically

Ⓑ Geographically

Ⓒ Randomly

Ⓓ Spatially

10. Which of the following is a supporting detail in this article?

Ⓐ Alaska's Iditarod Trail is the world's most famous sled dog racing venue

Ⓑ After the heroic journey of 1925, mushing became more popular

Ⓒ Some mushers run their dogs over 1,500 miles to prepare for the race

Ⓓ There are specific requirements to enter the Iditarod Trail race

11. What do participants receive at the first mushers' banquet?

Ⓐ Awards

Ⓑ Racing order numbers

Ⓒ Supplies

Ⓓ Trail maps

12. What is the interval used to separate mushers as they begin the Iditarod Trail race?

Ⓐ Five minutes

Ⓑ One minute

Ⓒ Ten minutes

Ⓓ Two minutes

Questions 13 –24 pertain to the following story:

The Right Thing to Do

Characters *(in order of appearance)*:
JESSICA—a sixth-grade girl, Amy's friend
GROUP OF FRIENDS—a group of sixth-grade girls
AMY—a sixth-grade girl, Jessica's friend
SALES CLERK—a clerk in the store Amy and Jessica visit

Scene 1

(1) *Jessica stands with a group of friends on the school steps. The group is chatting and laughing. Amy approaches from stage right.*
(2) AMY: Jessica! Jessica!
(3) JESSICA: *(turning away from her friends and taking a step toward Amy)* Hi, Amy. What's up?
(4) AMY: I'm headed to the mall, and I thought you might want to come.
(5) JESSICA: Why me? I thought we weren't friends anymore.
(6) AMY: *(waving her hand and shaking her head)* That old fight? Ancient history. So ... do you want to come or not?
(7) JESSICA: *(glancing back at her friends)* Sure. I'll come. Just give me a minute.
(8) *Jessica runs back and talks with her friends for a moment, then rejoins Amy. Amy and Jessica exit stage right.*

Scene 2

(9) *Amy and Jessica are looking at a shelf full of lipstick in a cosmetics store in the mall.*
(10) AMY: Look at this one, Jess. Don't you just love this color? *(She picks up a lipstick tube.)*
(11) JESSICA: It's nice, but I like this one better. *(She picks up a different tube of lipstick.)*
(12) *A sales clerk enters from stage left.*
(13) SALES CLERK: *(stopping by the girls)* Can I help you ladies find something?
(14) AMY: Oh, no. We're just looking.
(15) JESSICA: Thank you, though.
(16) SALES CLERK: Okay. Well, let me know if you need anything. *(He/she exits stage right.)*
(17) AMY: So, which one are you going to get?
(18) JESSICA: *(looking at the floor and shaking her head)* I'm not getting one. They're a little spendy for me. Besides, I'm saving up for something special.
(19) AMY: *(laughing)* Who said anything about money? *(She slips her favorite lipstick into her pocket.)* I didn't ask you which one you were going to buy. I asked which one you were going to get. So, which one will it be?
(20) JESSICA: But—but—that's stealing!
(21) AMY: Look at all these tubes of lipstick. They'll never miss a couple.
(22) JESSICA: *(looking around nervously)* What if that sales clerk comes back and catches us?
(23) AMY: You worry too much. *(She picks up two tubes of lipstick.)* Now, was this the one you liked? Or was it this one? Never mind. We'll take them both. *(She slips them both into her pocket.)*

- 23 -

(24) JESSICA: Amy! This is wrong. We shouldn't be doing this.
(25) AMY: *(glaring at Jessica)* Do you even want to be my friend again? It sure doesn't sound like it.
(26) JESSICA: Of course I want to be your friend. It's just—
(27) AMY: Then come on. Let's go. *(She starts to walk away, and then turns and looks back.)* Are you coming?
(28) JESSICA: Fine. *(She follows Amy.)* But what if the alarm goes off?
(29) AMY: For a couple of tubes of lipstick? Not gonna happen. Now, follow me. And for heaven's sake, don't look so nervous.
(30) *The girls exit stage right.*

Scene 3

(31) *Jessica reenters the cosmetics store from stage right. She stops at the shelf of lipsticks and looks around. The sales clerk enters from stage left.*
(32) JESSICA: Excuse me ...
(33) SALES CLERK: *(stopping)* Did you need help with something?
(34) JESSICA: Yes. *(She looks at the floor.)* My friend who was just with me, um, she took—well, actually, she stole three tubes of lipstick. I'm not okay with that. So, um, I wanted to pay for them.
(35) SALES CLERK: That's impressive. I've never seen that happen before. And kids take stuff from this store all the time. What made you come back?
(36) JESSICA: *(shrugging)* I don't know. I guess it was just the right thing to do.

13. In paragraph 6, what does Amy mean when she calls her fight with Jessica "ancient history"?

Ⓐ It happened thousands of years ago

Ⓑ It happened in history class

Ⓒ Amy has totally forgotten about the fight

Ⓓ They were arguing about events in ancient history

14. What is the setting for Scene 1?

Ⓐ The school steps

Ⓑ The mall

Ⓒ A cosmetics store

Ⓓ Amy's house

15. What is the setting for Scene 2 and Scene 3?

Ⓐ The school steps

Ⓑ Jessica's house

Ⓒ A cosmetics store

Ⓓ Amy's house

16. Which scene contains the climax of this play?

Ⓐ Scene 1

Ⓑ Scene 2

Ⓒ Scene 3

Ⓓ All of the above

17. Which scene contains the denouement of this play?

Ⓐ Scene 1

Ⓑ Scene 2

Ⓒ Scene 3

Ⓓ All of the above

18. In paragraph 29, why is the word "gonna" considered acceptable?

Ⓐ It shows Amy's pattern of slang speech

Ⓑ It is always acceptable in written English

Ⓒ It is a different language spoken by Amy

Ⓓ It is not acceptable; it is a misspelling

19. In paragraph 6, what type of figurative language is used when Amy says "ancient history"?

Ⓐ Metaphor

Ⓑ Simile

Ⓒ Personification

Ⓓ Hyperbole

20. Which of the following best describes the overall tone of this play?

Ⓐ Formal

Ⓑ Conversational

Ⓒ Classical

Ⓓ Musical

21. What is the underlying theme of this play?

Ⓐ Amy and Jessica are best friends

Ⓑ Doing the right thing is always a good decision

Ⓒ It is okay to steal if you are not caught

Ⓓ Shopping for cosmetics increases peer pressure

22. Which paragraph best shows Amy's justification for stealing the lipstick?

Ⓐ Paragraph 21

Ⓑ Paragraph 23

Ⓒ Paragraph 25

Ⓓ Paragraph 29

23. Why does Jessica say she is not buying lipstick?

Ⓐ She does not wear lipstick

Ⓑ She does not like any of the lipstick colors

Ⓒ She wants Amy to buy a lipstick for her

Ⓓ The lipstick is expensive, and she is saving her money

24. Which of the following is the best summary of this play?

Ⓐ Jessica leaves her other friends to be friends with Amy again, and she and Amy go to the mall

Ⓑ Amy teaches Jessica how to steal lipstick without getting caught, being a bad influence on Jessica

Ⓒ Jessica agrees to go to the mall with Amy, but when Amy steals lipstick, Jessica goes back to pay for it

Ⓓ Jessica thinks stealing is wrong, and she thinks Amy is a bad influence because she is a thief

Questions 25 – 36 pertain to the following two short stories:

The Talent Show

(1) The first notes floated from the piano. Megan smiled, warm and excited beneath the glaring stage lights. This was her moment. She had practiced. She had prepared. She was ready. As the introduction ended, Megan opened her mouth and began to sing.

(2) The song flowed along, and Megan relaxed, scanning the faces of the audience. But somewhere in the middle of the second verse, her mind suddenly went blank. The music went on, but the words were gone. Megan's

smile faded. She stood silently with her mouth hanging open. When the music finally trickled to a stop, Megan ran from the stage.

(3) In a cramped dressing room backstage, Megan buried her face in her hands. She had wanted so much to win this talent show. Tears seeped between her fingers. Her confidence and pride and excitement had been replaced by utter disappointment. She felt a hand on her shoulder and lifted her damp face.

(4) "Ella and Kaylee are here," Megan's mom said, giving her shoulder a quick squeeze.

(5) Ella and Kaylee, Megan's two best friends, pulled folding chairs over to face Megan. She looked at them forlornly.

(6) "I'm a total failure," she moaned.

(7) Ella and Kaylee exchanged glances. Kaylee reached out and squeezed Megan's hand.

(8) "What are you talking about?" Kaylee said. "That first verse was some of your best singing ever."

(9) "Thanks," Megan said. "But the problem is that the first verse is all I sang. Then I totally bombed. I can't believe I forgot the words after all that practice."

(10) "You didn't totally bomb," Ella said. "You just forgot the words. That happens to everybody. Besides, don't the pros say you should leave your audience wanting more?"

(11) "I guess so," Megan admitted.

(12) "Well, trust me," Ella said. "I guarantee they wanted more—like the rest of the song! You probably did, too."

(13) Megan smiled a little. "So, you guys don't think I'm a total dork for forgetting the words?"

(14) "Of course not," Kaylee said. "Forgetting the words doesn't make you a dork. It just makes you human. And you're still the most talented person I know."

(15) Ella nodded in agreement. Megan pulled Ella and Kaylee into a quick hug. Then she wiped her eyes and managed a genuine smile.

(16) "I'm so lucky to have best friends like you two," Megan said. "It's nice to know that you'll be my friends forever, no matter what!"

The Tournament

(1) Looking for a hole in the defense, Scott dribbled the ball, shifting it from hand to hand. A trickle of sweat ran down his back. No one was open. There were only seconds left on the clock, and Scott knew he had a difficult decision to make.

(2) The other team was leading by two points, and Scott was just outside the three-point line. If he could make the shot, the Eagles would be state champions again. But if he missed ... Scott didn't want to think about that. He knew what he had to do.

(3) It was a classic jump shot. The ball left his hands and sailed toward the basket in a perfect arc. The crowd, the other players, the whole stadium seemed frozen in time. All eyes were on the ball as it struck the rim and bounced off. The buzzer blared. The game was over. Scott had missed, and the Eagles had lost.

(4) Scott stood like a statue on the court as people surged around him. Elated family members swarmed the winning team. Teammates hugged and slapped each other on the back. Even Scott's own teammates joined in the celebration.

(5) Suddenly, Scott felt himself being hoisted unsteadily onto the shoulders of his friends. Over the loudspeaker, the announcer proclaimed that Scott had been named the most valuable player of the championship game. Everyone cheered, and the Eagles took a victory lap with Scott on their shoulders. Finally, Scott's friends put him back on solid ground.

(6) Scott was bewildered. He was the one who missed the most important shot of the game. How could anyone call him the most valuable player? He didn't feel very valuable at the moment. Scott approached Coach Travis.

(7) "Coach," Scott said, "there must be some mistake. I can't be the most valuable player."

(8) "There's no mistake," Coach Travis said. "You had 26 points, 11 rebounds, and 8 assists. I'd say that makes you a very valuable player."

(9) "But I missed that last shot," Scott said. "We lost the game because of me."

(10) "I don't know about that," said Coach Travis. "Everybody misses a shot from time to time. Don't be so hard on yourself. It's all about perspective."

(11) "What do you mean?" Scott asked.

(12) "Well," Coach Travis answered, "you could say you are the reason we lost the game because you missed that last shot. On the other hand, you could say you are the reason we almost won because of your awesome performance throughout the game. How you look at it is up to you."

(13) Scott's teammates came running over and surrounded Coach Travis. They jostled one another playfully, talking and laughing.

(14) "Hey, Coach," one player called out, "how about treating your team to pizza?"

(15) "I don't know," said Coach Travis. "Do you think you deserve pizza?"

(16) Scott piped up. "Of course we do! After all, we almost won the game."

(17) Coach Travis smiled. "You're right, Scott. We did almost win. Okay. Pizza for everyone!"

Questions 25-29 pertain to "The Talent Show" short story:

25. Which of the following is the best definition of "forlornly" as it is used in paragraph 5?

Ⓐ With a happy spirit

Ⓑ With a sad spirit

Ⓒ With a lonely spirit

Ⓓ With an angry spirit

26. What is the main theme of this story?

Ⓐ Real friends support you, no matter what

Ⓑ It is easy to forget the words of a song

Ⓒ Performing in a talent show can be embarrassing

Ⓓ Megan feels like a failure

27. What point of view is used to tell this story?

Ⓐ First person

Ⓑ Second person

Ⓒ Third person

Ⓓ None of the above

28. Which of the following is a supporting detail in this story?

Ⓐ Megan is singing in a talent show

Ⓑ Megan forgets the words of her song

Ⓒ Megan is disappointed in herself

Ⓓ Megan is accompanied by piano music

29. What does Kaylee do in paragraph 8 to try to make Megan feel better?

Ⓐ She makes a joke about Megan's performance

Ⓑ She compliments Megan on her singing

Ⓒ She tells about a time when she forgot a song

Ⓓ She sings a song with Megan

Questions 30-34 pertain to "The Tournament" short story:

30. In paragraph 4, what does "elated" mean?

Ⓐ Happy and excited

Ⓑ Frustrated and angry

Ⓒ Loud and rowdy

Ⓓ Pushy and proud

31. In the first sentence of paragraph 4, what type of figurative language is used?

Ⓐ Hyperbole

Ⓑ Metaphor

Ⓒ Personification

Ⓓ Simile

32. Which of the following best expresses the theme of this story?

Ⓐ The Eagles want to be the state champions

Ⓑ There are different ways to look at any situation

Ⓒ Winning isn't everything

Ⓓ Scott is a very good basketball player

33. Which of the following is the best summary of this story?

Ⓐ At the buzzer, Scott misses an important basket because he isn't a very good basketball player

Ⓑ Coach Travis feels Scott is the most valuable player in the game because he scored 26 points

Ⓒ When Scott misses an important shot, he is disappointed, but Coach Travis shows him there are different ways to look at the situation

Ⓓ The Eagles lose the state championship because of Scott, but Coach Travis sees things differently and makes Scott the most valuable player

34. Why is Scott so upset in this story?

Ⓐ He feels responsible for losing the game

Ⓑ He thinks he is a bad basketball player

Ⓒ He doesn't like Coach Travis

Ⓓ He doesn't want to play basketball anymore

Questions 35-36 pertain to both "The Talent Show" and "The Tournament" short stories:

35. In what ways are Scott and Megan most similar in these stories?

Ⓐ They are both performers.

Ⓑ They are both very active.

Ⓒ They are both disappointed in themselves.

Ⓓ They both have good friends.

36. What general theme is evident in both stories?

Ⓐ Winning is important, but it isn't everything

Ⓑ Good friends are the most valuable thing in life

Ⓒ Coaches can offer good perspective on tough situations

Ⓓ When you try your best, you shouldn't be disappointed in yourself

Questions 37-48 pertain to the following story:

Everybody's Problem

(1) I used to think homeless people were dirty and lazy and mean. I thought they were all old men with scraggly beards and mangy dogs. I thought they lived on the street because they wanted to. I thought they were all drug addicts and alcoholics who ate from garbage cans and slept in boxes. I used to think homelessness wasn't my problem. Then I met Chris, and he showed me I was wrong—about everything. Homelessness is everybody's problem.

(2) The sun was climbing into the bright blue sky as we loaded up the bus at the youth center. It was a crisp, cold Thanksgiving morning, and our youth group was headed down to a local shelter called The Lighthouse. We were going to serve Thanksgiving dinner to more than a hundred homeless people. It seemed like an appropriate way to spend Thanksgiving Day.

(3) When we arrived at the shelter, we were each given a job to do. My job was peeling potatoes. The shelter director gave me a peeler and a garbage can and sat me down in front of a giant pile of potatoes. I had never seen so many potatoes in one place before. They rose from the tray like Mt. Everest. By the time I had peeled them all, my hands and arms and shoulders ached.

(4) When the kitchen work was done, we were given our serving stations. The director explained that this was the only meal many of the homeless people would eat that day, and for some, it was the only hot meal they would have that week. Even so, there wasn't a lot of food for so many people. We were supposed to give each person one slice of turkey, one scoop of mashed potatoes, one scoop of stuffing, a small drizzle of gravy, a few green beans, and a sliver of pumpkin pie.

(5) I was plodding along, dishing up mashed potatoes with an ice cream scoop, when I happened to look up at the person I was serving. He wasn't a dirty, bearded old man. He was a boy about my age, with brown hair and brown eyes and a patched green jacket.

(6) "Hi," the boy said. "I'm Chris."

(7) "I'm Ben," I said as I scooped some potatoes onto his plate. "Happy Thanksgiving."

(8) "Thanks," Chris said, and then he was gone.

(9) As Chris moved down the line, I began to look around, really seeing things for the first time. Very few of the homeless people fit my stereotype. There were men and women, old and young. Children played in a corner of the dining room. At one table, teenagers talked in a tight group. People chatted and smiled. A few were even laughing. This was not what I had pictured a homeless shelter would be like.

- 31 -

(10) When everyone had been served, I began to help clean up. I couldn't help watching Chris as I cleared the tables and wiped them down. He was playing peek-a-boo with a little girl in a high chair. I wondered if it was his little sister.

(11) I was so lost in thought that I jumped when the shelter director tapped my shoulder. She laughed.

(12) "I'll finish cleaning up here," she said. "Why don't you go talk to Chris? He's very nice."

(13) As I approached the table where Chris was sitting, I felt nervous. What would I say? Could we possibly have anything to talk about? Would he even want to talk to me? I sat cautiously beside him.

(14) "Hi, Ben," he said.

(15) "Hi, Chris. Is that your little sister?"

(16) Chris smiled. "Yep. This is Sophia. And over there is my little brother, Dane." Chris motioned toward the corner where the smaller children were playing. Then he pointed to a dark-haired woman at a nearby table. "That's my mom."

(17) "Are you all homeless?" I asked.

(18) "Yep," answered Chris. "We've been here at The Lighthouse for almost two months now. It's okay here, but I miss my old school and my friends. I hope we can move back to a real house soon."

(19) "I didn't know there was such a thing as homeless kids," I admitted.

(20) "Me neither," said Chris. "At least, not until I became one."

(21) "How did it happen?" I asked. Then I had second thoughts. "I mean, you don't have to tell me if you don't want to. I was just wondering."

(22) "It's okay," Chris said. "I don't mind talking about it. About a year ago, my dad got really sick. He was in the hospital for a few months. Then he died. We didn't have any insurance or anything, and my mom couldn't get a job. Besides, she was really sad, and she was trying to take care of me and Dane and Sophia."

(23) "So, how did you end up homeless?" I wondered.

(24) "Mom says there were just too many bills and not enough money. First, we got our lights turned off. Then we couldn't pay our rent, so we had to move out of our house. We stayed with friends for a while, but eventually there was nobody left to stay with. So, we came here."

(25) "Will you stay here forever?" I asked.

(26) "No," Chris said. "My mom is in a program to give her training and help her get a job. When she finds a job, we can get a new place to live. Then things can be normal again."

(27) I heard my youth leader calling for us to load the bus. I wanted to talk to Chris more and ask him more questions, but I knew I had to leave. I stood up.

(28) "I have to go," I said. "I'm glad I got to meet you, Chris. I hope you get a new house soon."

(29) "Thanks, Ben," Chris said. "It was nice to meet you, too. Thanks for hanging out with me for a while. Happy Thanksgiving."

(30) "Happy Thanksgiving," I echoed as I headed toward the door. When I looked back, Chris waved. Then he started playing peek-a-boo with Sophia again.

(31) I will probably never see Chris again, but I have thought of him many times since that day. In just a few minutes together, he taught me so much

about the problem of homelessness. It isn't just a problem that affects lazy, mean old men. It affects men and women of all ages. It affects children. It affects whole families. It affected Chris. And because I got the chance to see homelessness through his eyes, it affects me now, too. I think I'll go back again next Thanksgiving … or maybe sooner. After all, now I know that homelessness is everybody's problem.

37. What is the setting for this story?

Ⓐ A youth center

Ⓑ A homeless shelter

Ⓒ A community center

Ⓓ A school

38. If you were describing this story, what classification would you use?

Ⓐ Memoir

Ⓑ Biography

Ⓒ Autobiography

Ⓓ Fiction

39. In paragraph 9, what does the word "stereotype" mean?

Ⓐ A textbook definition of a concept

Ⓑ Height, weight, and physical features

Ⓒ A generalized idea of what something is like

Ⓓ A description given by an authority figure

40. What point of view is used to tell this story?

Ⓐ First person

Ⓑ Second person

Ⓒ Third person

Ⓓ All of the above

41. What is the main theme of this story?

Ⓐ Kids can be homeless

Ⓑ Potatoes are difficult to peel

Ⓒ Serving at a homeless shelter is a good Thanksgiving project

Ⓓ Homelessness is everybody's problem

42. What does the author compare the potatoes to in paragraph 3?

Ⓐ A tower

Ⓑ A mountain range

Ⓒ Mt. Everest

Ⓓ A mound

43. Which of the following items was not included in the Thanksgiving dinner at the shelter?

Ⓐ Turkey

Ⓑ Cranberry sauce

Ⓒ Mashed potatoes and gravy

Ⓓ Pumpkin pie

44. What major event in the life of Chris's family led to their homelessness?

Ⓐ Their house burned down

Ⓑ Chris's mom lost her job

Ⓒ They had to live in their car

Ⓓ Chris's dad got sick and died

45. How does meeting Chris change Ben's mind about homelessness?

Ⓐ It doesn't change Ben's mind at all

Ⓑ It makes Ben afraid of being homeless

Ⓒ It helps Ben see that homelessness affects everyone

Ⓓ It keeps Ben from ever helping in a homeless shelter again

46. What do you think the author's primary purpose was in telling this story?

Ⓐ To persuade the reader to do something about homelessness

Ⓑ To inform the reader about The Lighthouse homeless shelter

Ⓒ To educate the reader on Thanksgiving service projects

Ⓓ To entertain the reader with a story about a personal experience

47. Which of the following is the best summary of this story?

Ⓐ In the beginning, Ben hates homeless people, but at the end, he loves them

Ⓑ Ben goes to a homeless shelter to serve Thanksgiving dinner and learns that homelessness affects everyone

Ⓒ The Lighthouse is a wonderful shelter that serves individuals and families who are homeless

Ⓓ Ben peels potatoes, serves food, meets Chris, and then goes home

48. Which of the following is Ben most likely to do in the future as a result of meeting Chris at The Lighthouse?

Ⓐ Avoid homeless people

Ⓑ Give away all his money

Ⓒ Try living on the street

Ⓓ Serve at a homeless shelter again

Answers and Explanations

TEKS Standard §110.18(b)(8)
1. B: A simile compares one thing to another by using "like" or "as"; the only simile in paragraph 1—"like a mirage"—refers to the path.

TEKS Standard §110.18(b)(2)(A)
2. C: "Landlocked" means "not on a waterway."

TEKS Standard §110.18(b)(7)
3. A: This information is found in Paragraph 5: "In March of 1973, the first Anchorage to Nome Iditarod Trail race was organized and held."

TEKS Standard §110.18(b)(10)(A)
4. D: This is an informational article – the author's main purpose in writing this article is to educate the reader about the Iditarod Trail.

TEKS Standard §110.18(b)(7)
5. D: The descriptive word "desperate" and the descriptive phrase "cry for help" are used in reference to the doctors in Nome in 1925.

TEKS Standard §110.18(b)(7)
6. A: Historical overviews, like this one, are best written in the third-person point of view.

TEKS Standard §110.18(b)(7)
7. C: We learn in Paragraph 5 that the Iditarod Trail became a National Historic Trail in 1978.

TEKS Standard §110.18(b)(10)(A)
8. B: This answer offers the most accurate summary of the history of the Iditarod Trail race.

TEKS Standard §110.18(b)(7)
9. A: This article is organized chronologically, from earliest to latest dates.

TEKS Standard §110.18(b)(10)(A)
10. C: is a supporting detail that expands on a main idea from the article. A, B, and D are not the best choices because they are all main points in the article instead of supporting details.

TEKS Standard §110.18(b)(7)
11. B: is We learn in Paragraph 7 that the race participants receive their racing order numbers at the first mushers' banquet.

TEKS Standard §110.18(b)(7)
12. D: We learn in Paragraph 8 that, as they begin the Iditarod Trail race, mushers are separated by two-minute intervals.

TEKS Standard §110.18(b)(2)
13. C: The phrase "ancient history" is a figure of speech. Amy uses it to communicate that she has totally forgotten about the fight.

TEKS Standard §110.18(b)(5)
14. A: Scene 1 is set on the school steps.

TEKS Standard §110.18(b)(5)
15. C: Scene 2 and Scene 3 take place in a cosmetics store.

TEKS Standard §110.18(b)(5) and (6)(A)
16. B: Scene 2 contains the climax of the play, when Jessica must decide whether to go along with Amy or not. In a story, the climax is the most exciting part of the story, when the action or tension builds to a zenith. This occurred when Jessica learned that Amy was planning on stealing the lipstick.

TEKS Standard §110.18(b)(5) and (6)(A)
17. C: Scene 3 contains the denouement of the play, when Jessica returns to the store to do the right thing. This is also known as the resolution of the story.

TEKS Standard §110.18(b)(6)(B)
18. A: The word "gonna" is used to show Amy's slang speech pattern.

TEKS Standard §110.18(b)(8)
19. D: The use of "ancient history" in paragraph 6 is a hyperbole, a major exaggeration.

TEKS Standard §110.18(b)(5)
20. B: The tone of this play is conversational.

TEKS Standard §110.18(b)(3)
21. B: The underlying theme of the play is that you should always do the right thing, even when it's difficult. This could also be called the moral of the story.

TEKS Standard §110.18(b)(5) and (6)(A)
22. A: In Paragraph 21, Amy tries to justify stealing the tubes of lipstick by saying that the store has a lot of them, and stealing only two or three of them won't do any harm because they won't even be missed.

TEKS Standard §110.18(b)(5)
23. D: In Paragraph 18, Jessica says the lipstick is too "spendy" for her, meaning it's too expensive, and she adds that she's trying to save money.

TEKS Standard §110.18(b)(6)(A)
24. C: is the most accurate and complete summary of the play.

TEKS Standard §110.18(b)(2)(A)
25. B: "Forlornly" is best defined as "with a sad spirit."

TEKS Standard §110.18(b)(3)(A)
26. A most accurately represents the main theme of the story.

TEKS Standard §110.18(b)(6)(C)

27. C: This story is written in the third person. That means the author is writing from the point of view of a narrator – someone who knows all the details of the story but isn't involved in it.

TEKS Standard §110.18(b)(10)(A)

28. D: is only option that offers a supporting detail, while the rest of the answer choices represent important parts of the story.

TEKS Standard §110.18(b)(6)

29. B: In paragraph 8, Kaylee compliments Megan's singing to help her feel better.

TEKS Standard §110.18(b)(2)(A)

30. A: If someone is "elated", they are extremely happy and excited about something.

TEKS Standard §110.18(b)(8)

31. D: The first sentence of paragraph 4 uses a simile when it says Scott "stood like a statue." A simile uses "like" or "as" to compare one thing to another.

TEKS Standard §110.18(b)(3)

32. B most clearly and completely expresses the theme of the story. Coach Travis tells Scott that "it's all about perspective", and then says that how Scott decides to look at it is up to him.

TEKS Standard §110.18(b)(6)(A)

33. C is the most complete and accurate summary of the story overall. A, B, and D are incorrect because they cover only part of the story or some of the main ideas and concepts.

TEKS Standard §110.18(b)(6)(A)

34. A: Scott is upset in the story because he feels responsible for the team's loss.

TEKS Standard §110.18(b)(10)(D)

35. C: Scott and Megan are most similar in their feelings of disappointment in themselves.

TEKS Standard §110.18(b)(3)(A) and (10)(D)

36. D: clearly reflects a general theme found in both stories.

TEKS Standard §110.18(b)(7)

37. B: This story is set at a homeless shelter.

TEKS Standard §110.18(b)(7)

38. A: This story is written in the style of a memoir, as evidenced by the first-person, reflective tone.

TEKS Standard §110.18(b)(2)(A)

39. C offers the best definition of "stereotype" as it is used in paragraph 9.

TEKS Standard §110.18(b)(6)(A) and (7)

40. A: This story is written in first person. That means the author is involved in the events of the story and is telling it from his point of view.

TEKS Standard §110.18(b)(3)

41. D: The main theme of the story is that homelessness is everybody's problem. One clue that this is the main point of the story is that the author clearly states it in the last line of the story. It's not always true that the last line of a short piece contains the main point, but that is often the case.

TEKS Standard §110.18(b)(7) and (8)

42. C: In paragraph 3 the author uses a simile to compare the size of the pile of potatoes to Mt. Everest.

TEKS Standard §110.18(b)(7)

43. B: Cranberry sauce was not served as part of the Thanksgiving dinner at the shelter.

TEKS Standard §110.18(b)(7)

44. D: The death of Chris's dad was the major problem the family had to deal with that eventually led to the their homelessness.

TEKS Standard §110.18(b)(7)

45. C: After meeting Chris, Ben had a completely different view of homelessness. Prior to the Thanksgiving meal, Ben thought homeless people were nothing but a bunch of old, filthy drunks and drug addicts. Meeting Ben and his family helped him understand that homelessness can happen to all kinds of people.

TEKS Standard §110.18(b)(7) and (11)

46. A: The author's intention in writing this piece is to persuade the reader to do something about homelessness.

TEKS Standard §110.18(b)(7) and (10)(A)

47. B is the most complete and accurate summary of the story.

TEKS Standard §110.18(b)(7)

48. D is the best choice because the last paragraph of the story indicates that Ben is likely to serve at a homeless shelter again soon.

Practice Test #2

Practice Questions

Questions 1 – 12 pertain to the following article:

The Trouble with Tests

(1) Lisa was a good student. She studied hard, diligently did her homework, and turned in assignments on time. Whenever she had to take a test, however, Lisa had a problem. Her hands began to sweat and her stomach began to churn. She felt dizzy and breathless and sick. As a result, Lisa couldn't focus and always did poorly on tests. Her grades suffered, and so did her confidence level.

(2) Lisa's problem is a common one. Often called test anxiety, it includes any unusual stress symptoms that occur during tests. Symptoms can be as mild as light nausea or headache, or as severe as vomiting or uncontrollable shaking. Millions of students deal with test anxiety every year, but few realize it can be improved through three simple steps.

(3) The first step to improving test anxiety is better study habits. Proper preparation is an important step to overcoming test anxiety. It is important to develop regular study times, avoiding last minute "cramming" for a test. Studying heavily on the day of or night before a test can actually increase test anxiety in most students. The better option is to devote at least a half-hour block of time to reviewing class materials each day. This can help embed information in the brain, making it more accessible at test time.

(4) Using memory games and tools is another way to improve study habits. Using these tools and games can help students better retain information. It also makes learning more fun, reducing stress levels. Flashcards with key points or ideas can be very helpful when used alone or with a study partner. Mnemonic devices—silly sayings to help students recall complex concepts—are also helpful tools for reducing stress and improving test performance. An example of a mnemonic device is "Every Good Boy Deserves Fudge" to help music students remember the note names for the lines of the treble clef staff (EGBDF).

(5) The second step to reducing test anxiety is to use relaxation techniques. The first relaxation technique that is useful for test anxiety is visualization. This involves choosing a favorite place or event. When test anxiety symptoms appear, students can close their eyes and visualize themselves in that favorite place or at that favorite event. The students should focus on sensory information—sights, sounds, smells, etc. This refocuses the attention of the brain and reduces anxiety.

(6) Another relaxation technique that works well for test anxiety is deep breathing. When the body is under stress, breathing becomes shallower, causing the heart rate to increase and the blood pressure to rise. Conscious deep breathing helps increase oxygen flow to the body, reducing the heart rate and blood pressure. To do deep breathing, simply draw air in through the nose for five seconds, and then release the air through the mouth,

blowing out steadily for five seconds. Done with eyes open or closed, deep breathing exercises reduce stress and relax the body.

(7) The third step to reducing test anxiety is positive self-talk. Often, test anxiety is the result of or is compounded by a lack of faith in abilities. Students can overcome this through positive self-talk and self-affirmation. Before each test, a student should repeat, "I can do this"—or some similar positive mantra—over and over. This can be done out loud or silently; either way, it creates a positive attitude and outlook that can reduce anxiety.

(8) The self-affirmation of celebrating success is a final key to overcoming test anxiety. Students should share test-taking victories with friends and loved ones. Students should also feel proud when they do well on a test. Every success is a blow to the obstacle of test anxiety. As with anything else, practice makes perfect, and celebrating success helps a student practice triumph over test anxiety.

(9) Test anxiety is a real problem, not an imagined issue or an excuse. It can be overcome, however, through three basic steps. First, students must use study tools and good habits for proper preparation. Second, students must use relaxation techniques—such as visualization and deep breathing—to help release stress from the body. Finally, students must engage in positive self-talk and celebrate successes to create an atmosphere of triumph. When all three of these steps are consistently practiced, test anxiety will become a thing of the past.

1. According to this article, what is test anxiety?

Ⓐ A hereditary psychological disease

Ⓑ Unusual stress symptoms that occur during tests

Ⓒ An allergy to stress that is triggered by tests

Ⓓ Headaches and nausea that occur after tests

2. What is a mnemonic device?

Ⓐ A silly saying used to help remember a complex concept

Ⓑ A tool that increases physical relaxation during a test

Ⓒ An old-fashioned torture device involving repeated testing

Ⓓ A tool for selecting answers on tests

3. What is the main purpose of this article?

Ⓐ To show that test anxiety is a common problem

Ⓑ To discuss Lisa's problems with test anxiety

Ⓒ To identify the symptoms of test anxiety

Ⓓ To identify potential solutions for test anxiety

4. What is the general tone of this article?

Ⓐ Entertaining

Ⓑ Persuasive

Ⓒ Informative

Ⓓ Fictional

5. Which of the following offers the best summary of this article?

Ⓐ Test anxiety is a common problem that can be improved through three simple steps

Ⓑ Lisa has test anxiety, and she needs to learn how to deal with it better

Ⓒ Relaxation techniques are the best method for preventing test anxiety

Ⓓ Good study habits are the best tools for preventing test anxiety

6. According to paragraph 3, what common study practice should be avoided?

Ⓐ Using flashcards

Ⓑ Studying with a partner

Ⓒ Last-minute studying

Ⓓ Overstudying

7. What is the first step to improving test anxiety?

Ⓐ Better study habits

Ⓑ Relaxation techniques

Ⓒ Self-affirmation and positive self-talk

Ⓓ Teamwork and study partners

8. What is the third step to reducing test anxiety?

Ⓐ Better study habits

Ⓑ Positive self-talk

Ⓒ Visualization

Ⓓ Relaxation techniques

9. Which of the following ideas is a supporting detail in this article?

Ⓐ Millions of students deal with test anxiety every year

Ⓑ Using memory games and tools improves study habits

Ⓒ Test anxiety is a real problem

Ⓓ "Every Good Boy Deserves Fudge" is an example of a study tool

10. What organizational pattern is used for this article?

Ⓐ Inverted pyramid

Ⓑ Proposition and support

Ⓒ Problem and solution

Ⓓ Simple exposition

11. What two specific relaxation techniques are discussed in this article?

Ⓐ Massage and deep breathing

Ⓑ Visualization and muscle tensing

Ⓒ Meditation and massage

Ⓓ Visualization and deep breathing

12. Which paragraph discusses the "final key" to overcoming test anxiety?

Ⓐ Paragraph 6

Ⓑ Paragraph 8

Ⓒ Paragraph 7

Ⓓ Paragraph 9

Questions 13-17 pertain to the following poem:

Fog

(1) Stealthy fog drifts through the air,
(2) A dense, gray blanket everywhere.
(3) It slowly seeps in from the sea,
(4) Clutching rooftops, climbing trees.

(5) Its eerie whisper fills the land—
(6) "Catch me, catch me, if you can!"
(7) It skims the sky and hugs the ground,
(8) Distorts the vision, muffles sound.

(9) It fills the mind and fools the feet
(10) Like haunting shadows in the street.
(11) It creeps across the alleyway
(12) And dims the newborn light of day.

(13) It smothers landscapes without shame
(14) Then fades as quickly as it came.

13. Which of the following is the best synonym for "stealthy"?

Ⓐ Evil

Ⓑ Careful

Ⓒ Sneaky

Ⓓ Thick

14. What type of figurative language is used in line 5?

Ⓐ Personification

Ⓑ Metaphor

Ⓒ Simile

Ⓓ Hyperbole

15. What does the poet accomplish by using figurative language throughout this poem?

Ⓐ The poet meets the basic requirements of poetry

Ⓑ The poet makes the fog seem alive

Ⓒ The poet confuses and overwhelms the reader

Ⓓ The poet gives additional length to the poem

16. To what is the fog compared in line 2?

Ⓐ A whisper

Ⓑ The sea

Ⓒ A shadow

Ⓓ A blanket

17. Which of the following best describes the rhyming pattern of this poem?

Ⓐ ABAB CDCD EFEF GG

Ⓑ AAAA BBBB CCCC DD

Ⓒ ABCD EFGH IJKL MN

Ⓓ AABB CCDD EEFF GG

Questions 18 – 22 pertain to the following poem:

Summer Afternoon

(1) Golden sunlight bathes the meadow
(2) In brilliant midday glory.
(3) Slim green pillars bow in homage
(4) To a gentle summer breeze.
(5) Flowers turn their eager faces
(6) Upward to an azure sky.
(7) All is quiet, calm, and peaceful,
(8) Dozing in the pleasant heat.

(9) Just across the sleepy meadow
(10) A lazy stream meanders through,
(11) Sauntering between the banks
(12) Of hardened, sun-baked earth.
(13) Dragonflies flit to and fro
(14) Like scattered thoughts and fleeting dreams.
(15) Bright light glistens on the water
(16) Like sparkling, molten silver.

(17) The meadow rests in tacit glow
(18) As minutes turn to hours.
(19) The sun sinks lower in the sky,
(20) And shadows slowly lengthen.
(21) Daylight, dappled by the trees,
(22) Spreads across the open landscape
(23) Like a dim and dusky cloak,
(24) And—in silence—evening falls.

18. What do lines 3 and 4 refer to in a metaphor?

Ⓐ Green buildings in the field

Ⓑ Grasses waving in the wind

Ⓒ Trees waving in the wind

Ⓓ People worshipping the wind

19. What type of figurative language is used in lines 13 and 14?

Ⓐ Simile

Ⓑ Metaphor

Ⓒ Hyperbole

Ⓓ Personification

20. What does "tacit" mean in line 17?

Ⓐ Beautiful

Ⓑ Lazy

Ⓒ Silent

Ⓓ Bored

21. Which of the following best describes the mood of this poem?

Ⓐ Upbeat and exciting

Ⓑ Quiet and peaceful

Ⓒ Depressing and sullen

Ⓓ Happy and energetic

22. How many stanzas does this poem contain?

Ⓐ 1

Ⓑ 8

Ⓒ 3

Ⓓ 24

Questions 23 -24 pertain to both "Fog" and "Summer Afternoon":
23. What general theme is represented in both of these poems?

ⒶNature

ⒷWater

ⒸEmotions

ⒹTime

24. What is the most important difference in the style of these two poems?

ⒶOne uses figurative language and the other does not

ⒷOne is longer than the other

ⒸOne is set at night and the other is set in the daytime

ⒹOne is rhymed and the other is free verse

Questions 25 – 36 pertain to the following story:

The Memory Quilt

(1) Kevin had been saving his allowance for months to buy a new bike. Now he was within a few dollars of his goal, and Grandma Ruth had offered to pay him to clean out her attic. Kevin was excited. The new bike was practically his!

(2) Early Saturday morning, Kevin's mom dropped him off at Grandma Ruth's house. Grandma Ruth hugged him. Then she walked upstairs with him and pointed him to a narrow ladder that led up to the attic.

(3) "It's a mess up there," she warned. "If you have any questions about anything, just ask. Most of it is old junk, though. You can sort things I won't want to keep into two piles—one to throw away and the other to donate to charity."

(4) Kevin climbed the ladder and looked around. Boxes and piles of old pictures and records and clothes littered the floor. It was a big job. He picked up a painting of flowers in a chipped wooden frame. It didn't look important, but Kevin thought he should check.

(5) "Grandma Ruth," he called, climbing down the ladder with the picture. "Is this important?"

(6) Grandma Ruth came out of her room and chuckled. "No, Kevin. Your grandfather and I bought that old picture at a yard sale years ago. Put it in the pile to donate to charity."

(7) Kevin climbed back up the ladder. He put the picture on the floor to start a pile for charity. Then he picked up an old, rusty toolbox. Like the old picture, it didn't look important, but Kevin thought he should check, just to make sure.

(8) "Grandma Ruth," he called again, climbing down the ladder with the toolbox. "Is this important?"

(9) Grandma Ruth laughed gently. "No, Kevin. Your grandfather bought that toolbox when we bought this old house. He was quite the handyman. But I have no use for it now. Put it in the pile to donate. And Kevin?"

(10) "Yes, Grandma Ruth?"

(11) "You don't have to check with me about each thing. If it looks old and unused, you can donate it or throw it away. I trust your judgment. But you can still ask if you have any questions." She winked at Kevin and went back into her room.

(12) Kevin climbed back up the ladder. He sorted through the piles quickly. By lunchtime, he was almost halfway done. He climbed down and ate tuna fish sandwiches with Grandma Ruth in the dining room. After lunch, she gave him some boxes to take up to the attic. She told him to box up and carry down the items to be donated to charity.

(13) Kevin made his way awkwardly back to the attic, carrying the boxes. He packed things up and sorted through piles until just before 4 pm, when his mom was coming to pick him up. The last item he grabbed was a faded, dusty quilt. He turned it over and studied it carefully. It was worn, and it seemed like it hadn't been used in a long time. Kevin threw it into a charity box and closed the top. Then he began carrying boxes down the ladder.

(14) Kevin's mom drove him by the Goodwill store on the way home. Together they unloaded the boxes of items to be donated. Then they headed home, where Kevin fell asleep right after dinner. He was exhausted from his hard work.

(15) Sunday afternoon, Kevin went back to Grandma Ruth's house to finish cleaning out the attic. The piles were sparser now, but they still popped up from the dusty floor like wayward molehills. He got right to work, sorting, boxing things up, and neatly stacking the items to be kept.

(16) Halfway through the afternoon, Grandma Ruth called Kevin down for cookies and milk.

(17) "Kevin, have you seen my old patchwork quilt up in the attic?" Grandma Ruth asked. "I can't seem to find it anywhere. I made that quilt from your grandfather's old work shirts and your mom's first baby blanket and the tablecloth I got at my wedding. There are so many memories in that quilt."

(18) Kevin gulped. He didn't want to lie to Grandma Ruth, but he couldn't tell her he donated her precious quilt to charity. She would kill him!

(19) "I'll look for it when I go back up," he promised, knowing it wasn't there.

(20) At the end of the afternoon, Kevin was done cleaning the attic. He carried the last box down the ladder.

(21) "Did you see my quilt up there?" Grandma Ruth asked.

(22) "No," Kevin said, half-truthfully.

(23) "I wonder where it could be," Grandma Ruth said.

(24) When Kevin and his mom stopped at the Goodwill store to donate the last set of boxes, Kevin asked if he could run inside. He dashed in and browsed the shelves carefully. Then he saw it. It was stuffed between two stacks of throw pillows. It was almost hidden, but unmistakable. He pulled out the quilt and checked the price.

(25) Kevin's heart fell. Paying for the quilt would mean he would have to wait another month or two to buy his bike. If he just went home, no one would ever know about his mistake. But he knew that would be wrong.

Buying the quilt back was the right thing to do. Kevin paid for the quilt and hurried back to the car.

(26) Kevin's mom looked at the quilt with surprise. "Isn't that Grandma Ruth's memory quilt?"

(27) Kevin nodded glumly. He told his mom the whole story. Then he said he needed to go back to Grandma Ruth's house to tell her the truth.

(28) "I'm proud of you," Kevin's mom said as she turned the car around. "Let's go give Grandma Ruth back her memories."

25. Which of the following is the best definition of "littered" as it is used in paragraph 4?

Ⓐ Stacked neatly on

Ⓑ Scattered across

Ⓒ Piled on

Ⓓ Put in a few places

26. What is the primary setting for this story?

Ⓐ Grandma Ruth's attic

Ⓑ The Goodwill store

Ⓒ Kevin's house

Ⓓ Grandma Ruth's dining room

27. In paragraph 15, what does "sparser" mean?

Ⓐ Denser

Ⓑ Larger and higher

Ⓒ Fewer and smaller

Ⓓ More organized

28. What point of view is used to tell this story?

Ⓐ First person

Ⓑ Second person

Ⓒ Third person

Ⓓ All of the above

29. What type of figurative language is used in paragraph 15?

Ⓐ Metaphor

Ⓑ Personification

Ⓒ Hyperbole

Ⓓ Simile

30. What is the general theme of this story?

Ⓐ Help your grandmother

Ⓑ Cleaning is best done in an organized way

Ⓒ Do the right thing

Ⓓ Never throw away or donate old items

31. Which paragraph contains the climax of this story?

Ⓐ Paragraph 12

Ⓑ Paragraph 16

Ⓒ Paragraph 24

Ⓓ Paragraph 25

32. Why was the quilt so valuable to Grandma Ruth?

Ⓐ It contained fabric from memorable things

Ⓑ It was sewn by hand by her grandmother

Ⓒ She had used the quilt for many years

Ⓓ It was a wedding present from Kevin's grandfather

33. Which of the following is a supporting detail in this story?

Ⓐ Kevin was saving his allowance for a new bike

Ⓑ Kevin and Grandma Ruth ate tuna fish sandwiches

Ⓒ Kevin was cleaning out Grandma Ruth's attic

Ⓓ Kevin donated Grandma Ruth's quilt to charity

34. Which of the following is the best summary of this story?

Ⓐ Kevin spends his Saturday cleaning out Grandma Ruth's attic so he can buy a bike

Ⓑ While cleaning out Grandma Ruth's attic, Kevin donates an important quilt to charity and has to get it back

Ⓒ Grandma Ruth describes her memory quilt to Kevin while eating cookies and milk

Ⓓ Kevin and his mom take Grandma Ruth's memory quilt back to her after finding it and buying it at Goodwill

35. Which of the following elements was not part of the memory quilt?

Ⓐ Grandma Ruth's wedding dress

Ⓑ Grandfather's old work shirts

Ⓒ Kevin's mom's baby blanket

Ⓓ Grandma Ruth's tablecloth

36. What type of figurative language is used at the end of paragraph 18?

Ⓐ Simile

Ⓑ Metaphor

Ⓒ Personification

Ⓓ Hyperbole

Questions 37 – 48 pertain to the following article:

Like Riding a Kite

(1) Imagine soaring high above the earth. There is no engine, no fuselage beneath you. There is only you, your glider, the wind, and the sky. It's like riding a kite with no strings attached, rising and falling on the breeze like a bird. It is freedom and thrill and ultimate pleasure. This is the world of hang gliding.

(2) While many people have a general idea of what hang gliding is all about, few really understand the sport. Most people don't realize a majestic glider can be collapsed to the size of a duffel bag. Few people know that gliders can stay aloft for hours and that the world distance record for a single glider flight is nearly 190 miles. Even fewer people realize that a hang glider can actually climb in the sky, even without an engine. In California, in the 1980s, one expert glider pilot gained more than 14,000 feet of altitude after takeoff! Hang gliders have mind-boggling capabilities.

(3) The amazing sport of hang gliding has a rich history dating back to the 1890s. In 1891, the first hang glider was invented by Otto Lilienthal in Germany. It was made of wood and cloth, weighed 40 pounds, was 23 feet wide, and could go about 35 miles per hour (mph) at an altitude of 100 feet. British inventor Percy Picher also built gliders with similar features in the

late 1890s. Unfortunately, both inventors were killed in glider crashes before their designs were perfected. With the element of danger involved in early hang gliding—and with the advent of airplane flight by the Wright brothers in 1903—many people lost interest in hang gliding.

(4) After the end of World War II, however, many military-trained pilots wanted to keep flying. Airplanes were too expensive for most people, so the sport of hang gliding was reborn. Through invention and innovation, new designs for hang gliders began to emerge. These included new materials and designs for glider construction and the addition of a control bar to improve safety. The basic design for today's hang gliders premiered at a meet in California in 1971. It included a broad, flexible wing on a sturdy frame with a control bar and a seat or safety harness.

(5) Since 1971, few major design changes have been made to hang gliders, although as new materials for construction become available, minor changes are made to improve flight. Modern sails range from 13 to 28 feet across. They are made of durable, lightweight, manmade fabric—such as nylon— and are designed to flex in shape and tension based on the wind. The sail is attached to a frame made from aluminum tubing. The frame includes a control bar, shaped like a rounded triangle and used for steering. Suspended from the frame is a harness or seat to improve pilot comfort and safety.

(6) Another way pilots improve comfort and safety is through the use of proper gear and equipment. Pilots should wear light, protective clothing and gloves designed for hang gliding. A helmet is also an important safety component. In addition, pilots need special instruments that are used during flight. These tools help measure thermals, the warm air currents used to lift and propel gliders through the air.

(7) Thermals are important to both taking off and staying aloft, but they aren't the only factor in flight. Modern gliders weigh about 35 pounds and are special balanced to a pilot's weight and preferences. To take off, the pilot is secured in the glider and then runs off the edge of a large hill or cliff, where thermals catch the glider and lift it into the air. If the wind is sustained at 12 mph or above, the pilot may even be able to take off without running. Once the glider is airborne, the pilot steers by shifting his/her weight and using the control bar. Each glider has its own unique feel, and a pilot must know the glider well to achieve a safe takeoff, flight, and landing.

(8) In addition to knowing the unique feel of the glider, a pilot must know the safety rules of the sky to have a safe flight. Pilots of hang gliders do not need to be licensed, but they must obey all rules and laws for flying. Hang glider pilots should never fly in bad weather or high winds. They must yield the right of way to any aircraft in distress and all hot air balloons. They must never intentionally fly into a cloud or a flock of birds. Finally, hang glider pilots should stay at least five miles away from airports during flight and at least 100 feet from buildings, telephone wires and poles, populated places, and crowds.

(9) Throughout history, mankind has looked for a way to soar with the birds across the canvas of the sky. Hang gliding offers that opportunity. With modern features and equipment, and with proper training in techniques and the rules of the sky, hang glider pilots can safely experience the thrill of flight. In a glider, the pilot is one with the breeze, the sunlight, the world

itself. Hang gliding is truly like riding a kite through the expanse of the heavens.

37. In paragraph 3, what does "advent" mean?

Ⓐ End

Ⓑ Beginning

Ⓒ Expansion

Ⓓ Popularity

38. Which of the following is the best definition of "thermals" as it is used in this article?

Ⓐ Protective clothing for pilots

Ⓑ Aluminum tubing used in glider frames

Ⓒ Tools used by pilots for safety

Ⓓ Warm air currents that lift gliders

39. What was the author's main purpose in writing this article?

Ⓐ To inform

Ⓑ To entertain

Ⓒ To analyze

Ⓓ To persuade

40. What type of figurative language is used in the first sentence of paragraph 9?

Ⓐ No figurative language is used in the first sentence of paragraph 9

Ⓑ Simile

Ⓒ Metaphor

Ⓓ Hyperbole

41. From what point of view is this article written?

Ⓐ First person

Ⓑ Second person

Ⓒ Third person

Ⓓ All of the above

42. Which of the following best describes the theme of this article?

Ⓐ Hang gliding has a rich history that began in the 1890s with two inventors

Ⓑ Modern hang gliding has come far and is a safe, fun way to soar through the sky

Ⓒ Hang gliders are 13 to 28 feet wide and have a sturdy frame and harness or seat

Ⓓ The modern hang glider premiered at a meet in California in 1971

43. What material is used to make modern hang glider frames?

Ⓐ Aluminum

Ⓑ Steel

Ⓒ Wood

Ⓓ PVC

44. Who invented the first hang glider in 1891?

Ⓐ Percy Picher

Ⓑ The Wright brothers

Ⓒ Donald Regalo

Ⓓ Otto Lilienthal

45. Which of the following is a main idea in this article?

Ⓐ Modern glider sails are 13 to 28 feet wide

Ⓑ Glider pilots must know the rules of the sky

Ⓒ All glider pilots should wear helmets for safety

Ⓓ Modern glider design premiered in 1971

46. How did World War II positively impact the sport of hang gliding?

Ⓐ It did not positively impact the sport of hang gliding

Ⓑ Gliders were used in World War II in Europe and Asia

Ⓒ Returning military pilots wanted to fly but couldn't afford planes

Ⓓ Flight had become much safer due to World War II technology

47. What is the minimum sustained wind speed for a hang glider pilot to take off without running?

Ⓐ 12 mph

Ⓑ 21 mph

Ⓒ 33 mph

Ⓓ 47 mph

48. How far away from airports should hang glider pilots stay while flying?

Ⓐ 100 feet

Ⓑ 500 feet

Ⓒ 1 mile

Ⓓ 5 miles

Answers and Explanations

TEKS Standard §110.18(b)(10)(A)
1. B: In paragraph 1, we learn that Lisa does poorly on tests because she suffers from a variety of unusual symptoms whenever she takes a test. In paragraph 2, the author tells us that there's a name for this condition, which is test anxiety.

TEKS Standard §110.18(b)(10)
2. A: The explanation of a mnemonic device is found in paragraph 4.

TEKS Standard §110.18(b)(10)(A)
3. D: The main purpose of this article is to identify potential solutions for test anxiety. The passage starts out by describing what test anxiety is, and then goes on to explain three ways to overcome it.

TEKS Standard §110.18(b)(10)
4. C: The tone of this article is informative. It's not fictional, and it's not trying to entertain readers, or persuade them to do something. It simply gives people information about what test anxiety is, and what they can do about it if they suffer from it.

TEKS Standard §110.18(b)(10)(A)
5. A: This answer choice offers the best summary of the article.

TEKS Standard §110.18(b)(10)(A)
6. C: According to paragraph 3, last-minute studying should be avoided.

TEKS Standard §110.18(b)(10)(A)
7. A: We learn in paragraph 3 that the first step to reducing test anxiety is better study habits.

TEKS Standard §110.18(b)(10)(A)
8. B: Paragraph 7 says the third step to reducing test anxiety is positive self-talk.

TEKS Standard §110.18(b)(10)(A)
9. D: This is the only answer choice that is a supporting detail. In other words, it represents a minor point of the article. A, B, and C are incorrect because they all represent main ideas in the article, not supporting details.

TEKS Standard §110.18(b)(10)(C)
10. C: This article is organized in a problem-and-solution format.

TEKS Standard §110.18(b)(10)(A)
11. D: Two specific relaxation techniques mentioned in the article are visualization and deep breathing. They can be found in paragraphs 5 and 6.

TEKS Standard §110.18(b)(10)(A)
12. B: Paragraph 8 discusses the "final key" to overcoming test anxiety.

TEKS Standard §110.18(b)(2)(A)
13. C: The word *sneaky* has almost the same meaning as *stealthy*, which means "quietly and secretly." When someone is doing something stealthily, they are trying to do something without been seen or heard.

TEKS Standard §110.18(b)(4)
14. A: Personification is using language that attributes human characteristics to non-human things. Line 5 uses personification when it suggests that the fog has an "eerie whisper."

TEKS Standard §110.18(b)(4)
15. B: The poet has filled this poem with figurative language to give the reader the impression that the fog is a living, breathing, thinking creature.

TEKS Standard §110.18(b)(4)
16. D: In line 2, the fog is compared to a "dense, gray blanket."

TEKS Standard §110.18(b)(4)
17. D: The rhyming pattern of this poem is AABB CCDD EEFF GG.

TEKS Standard §110.18(b)(4)
18. B: The metaphor in lines 3 and 4 refers to grasses waving in the wind.

TEKS Standard §110.18(b)(4)
19. A: Lines 13 and 14 contain a simile comparing the dragonflies to "scattered thoughts and fleeting dreams."

TEKS Standard §110.18(b)(2)(A) and (2)(B)
20. C: In line 17, "tacit" means silent.

TEKS Standard §110.18(b)(4)
21. B: The mood of this poem is quiet and peaceful. The author creates this mood by carefully choosing words, phrases, and rhythms to bring about these feelings in the reader.

TEKS Standard §110.18(b)(4)
22. C: This poem contains 3 stanzas. A stanza is a lot of sentences grouped together. In a poem, a stanza functions like a paragraph does in a prose piece.

TEKS Standard §110.18(b)(3)
23. A: Even though the poems are about two different subjects, fog and a summer afternoon, the general theme of both poems is nature.

TEKS Standard §110.18(b)(4)
24. D: The most important difference between the styles of these two poems is that one is rhymed and the other is free verse.

TEKS Standard §110.18(b)(2)(A) and (2)(B)

25. B: This is the correct answer because "scattered across" is the best definition of "littered" as it is used in paragraph 4. The author is trying to communicate that in Kevin's mind, junk was "all over the floor."

TEKS Standard §110.18(b)(6)

26. A: Some scenes take place in other places, but the main setting for this story is Grandma Ruth's attic, because that's where the bulk of the story actually takes place.

TEKS Standard §110.18(b)(2)(A) and (2)(B)

27. C: The phrase "fewer and smaller" is a good definition for "sparser" as it is used in paragraph 15. Kevin could see that he was making progress because there were fewer piles of junk left, and the ones that remained were smaller than they had been.

TEKS Standard §110.18(b)(6)(C)

28. C: This story is written in third-person point of view. That means it's being told about the characters in the story, not by any of them. If it had been written as if Kevin or his grandmother were telling the story, it would be in the first-person.

TEKS Standard §110.18(b)(8)

29. D: In paragraph 15 the piles of junk are compared to mole hills using "like," making the comparison a simile.

TEKS Standard §110.18(b)(3)(A)

30. C: The general theme of this story is "do the right thing." Even though it will cost Kevin some money, and it will mean that he will have to go without a new bike for several more weeks, he goes back to the store and purchases the quilt that meant so much to his grandmother.

TEKS Standard §110.18(b)(6)(A)

31. D: Paragraph 25 contains the climax of the story, when Kevin faces a moral dilemma, and must decide whether he will use his money for the quilt or save it for his bike.

TEKS Standard §110.18(b)(6)

32. A: In paragraph 17, Grandma Ruth tells Kevin that the quilt held so many important memories for her.

TEKS Standard §110.18(b)(6) and (10)(A)

33. B: This answer choice is the only one that is a supporting detail. The fact that they had tuna sandwiches for lunch doesn't mean much to the overall story. The other answer choices represent things that are important to the development of the story.

TEKS Standard §110.18(b)(6) and (10)(A)

34. B: This is the most clear and accurate summary of the story.

TEKS Standard §110.18(b)(6)

35. A: Grandma Ruth's memory quilt did not include pieces from her wedding dress. The other three answer choices are all elements that were part of Grandma Ruth's memory quilt. This information is found in paragraph 17.

TEKS Standard §110.18(b)(6) and (8)
36. D: Hyperbole is exaggeration. Kevin knew that his grandmother would be very upset if she found out that he had thrown out the quilt, but he also knew that there was no way she was going to actually kill him. That was hyperbole.

TEKS Standard §110.18(b)(2)(A) and (2)(B)
37. B: The word *advent* means "beginning."

TEKS Standard §110.18(b)(2)(A) and (2)(B)
38. D: is the best choice because in this article, *thermals* are warm air currents that lift gliders. The definition of the word can be found in paragraph 6: "These tools help measure thermals, the warm air currents used to lift and propel gliders through the air."

TEKS Standard §110.18(b)(10)
39. A: The author's main purpose in writing this article is to tell the reader about hang gliding – how long it's been taking place, how it got started, how it works, some rules and safety guidelines, etc.

TEKS Standard §110.18(b)(8)
40. C: The first sentence of paragraph 9 uses a metaphor to compare the sky to a canvas.

TEKS Standard §110.18(b)(6)(C)
41. C: This article is written in third-person point of view. If the author were talking about his own experiences, using words such as *I* and *me*, then it would be in the first-person.

TEKS Standard §110.18(b)(3)
42. B: is the best choice because it offers the most accurate description of the theme of the article. A, C, and D are all points mentioned in the passage, but they do not accurately and completely describe the theme of the article.

TEKS Standard §110.18(b)(10)
43. A: Modern hang glider frames are made from aluminum. This information can be found in paragraph 5.

TEKS Standard §110.18(b)(10)
44. D: Paragraph 3 says that Otto Lilienthal invented the first hang glider in 1891.

TEKS Standard §110.18(b)(10)(A)
45. B: This is the only option that represents a main idea of the article. A, C, and D are not the best choices because they are all supporting details, not main ideas of the article.

TEKS Standard §110.18(b)(10)
46. C: Paragraph 4 says that hang gliding experienced a revival of interest after World War II, when many military pilots were frustrated after coming home from the war, because they couldn't afford to fly planes, so they took up hang gliding.

TEKS Standard §110.18(b)(10)
47. A: Paragraph 7 says the minimum sustained wind speed for a glider pilot to take off without running is 12 mph.

TEKS Standard §110.18(b)(10)

48. D: Paragraph 8 says hang glider pilots should stay five miles away from airports while flying.

Success Strategies

The most important thing you can do is to ignore your fears and jump into the test immediately- do not be overwhelmed by any strange-sounding terms. You have to jump into the test like jumping into a pool- all at once is the easiest way.

Make Predictions

As you read and understand the question, try to guess what the answer will be. Remember that several of the answer choices are wrong, and once you begin reading them, your mind will immediately become cluttered with answer choices designed to throw you off. Your mind is typically the most focused immediately after you have read the question and digested its contents. If you can, try to predict what the correct answer will be. You may be surprised at what you can predict.

Quickly scan the choices and see if your prediction is in the listed answer choices. If it is, then you can be quite confident that you have the right answer. It still won't hurt to check the other answer choices, but most of the time, you've got it!

Answer the Question

It may seem obvious to only pick answer choices that answer the question, but the test writers can create some excellent answer choices that are wrong. Don't pick an answer just because it sounds right, or you believe it to be true. It MUST answer the question. Once you've made your selection, always go back and check it against the question and make sure that you didn't misread the question, and the answer choice does answer the question posed.

Benchmark

After you read the first answer choice, decide if you think it sounds correct or not. If it doesn't, move on to the next answer choice. If it does, mentally mark that answer choice. This doesn't mean that you've definitely selected it as your answer choice, it just means that it's the best you've seen thus far. Go ahead and read the next choice. If the next choice is worse than the one you've already selected, keep going to the next answer choice. If the next choice is better than the choice you've already selected, mentally mark the new answer choice as your best guess.

The first answer choice that you select becomes your standard. Every other answer choice must be benchmarked against that standard. That choice is correct until proven otherwise by another answer choice beating it out. Once you've decided that no other answer choice seems as good, do one final check to ensure that your answer choice answers the question posed.

Valid Information

Don't discount any of the information provided in the question. Every piece of information may be necessary to determine the correct answer. None of the information in the question is there to throw you off (while the answer choices will certainly have information to throw you off). If two seemingly unrelated topics are discussed, don't ignore either. You can be confident there is a relationship, or it wouldn't be included in the question, and you are probably going to have to determine what is that relationship to find the answer.

Avoid "Fact Traps"

Don't get distracted by a choice that is factually true. Your search is for the answer that answers the question. Stay focused and don't fall for an answer that is true but incorrect. Always go back to the question and make sure you're choosing an answer that actually answers the question and is not just a true statement. An answer can be factually correct, but it MUST answer the question asked. Additionally, two answers can both be seemingly correct, so be sure to read all of the answer choices, and make sure that you get the one that BEST answers the question.

Milk the Question

Some of the questions may throw you completely off. They might deal with a subject you have not been exposed to, or one that you haven't reviewed in years. While your lack of knowledge about the subject will be a hindrance, the question itself can give you many clues that will help you find the correct answer. Read the question carefully and look for clues. Watch particularly for adjectives and nouns describing difficult terms or words that you don't recognize. Regardless of if you completely understand a word or not, replacing it with a synonym either provided or one you more familiar with may help you to understand what the questions are asking. Rather than wracking your mind about specific detailed information concerning a difficult term or word, try to use mental substitutes that are easier to understand.

The Trap of Familiarity

Don't just choose a word because you recognize it. On difficult questions, you may not recognize a number of words in the answer choices. The test writers don't put "make-believe" words on the test; so don't think that just because you only recognize all the words in one answer choice means that answer choice must be correct. If you only recognize words in one answer choice, then focus on that one. Is it correct? Try your best to determine if it is correct. If it is, that is great, but if it doesn't, eliminate it. Each word and answer choice you eliminate increases your chances of getting the question correct, even if you then have to guess among the unfamiliar choices.

Eliminate Answers

Eliminate choices as soon as you realize they are wrong. But be careful! Make sure you consider all of the possible answer choices. Just because one appears right, doesn't mean that the next one won't be even better! The test writers will usually put more than one good answer choice for every question, so read all of them. Don't worry if you are stuck between two that seem right. By getting down to just two remaining possible choices, your odds are now 50/50. Rather than wasting too much time, play the odds. You are guessing, but guessing wisely, because you've been able to knock out some of the answer choices that you know are wrong. If you are eliminating choices and realize that the last answer choice you are left with is also obviously wrong, don't panic. Start over and consider each choice again. There may easily be something that you missed the first time and will realize on the second pass.

Tough Questions

If you are stumped on a problem or it appears too hard or too difficult, don't waste time.

Move on! Remember though, if you can quickly check for obviously incorrect answer choices, your chances of guessing correctly are greatly improved. Before you completely give up, at least try to knock out a couple of possible answers. Eliminate what you can and then guess at the remaining answer choices before moving on.

Brainstorm

If you get stuck on a difficult question, spend a few seconds quickly brainstorming. Run through the complete list of possible answer choices. Look at each choice and ask yourself, "Could this answer the question satisfactorily?" Go through each answer choice and consider it independently of the other. By systematically going through all possibilities, you may find something that you would otherwise overlook. Remember that when you get stuck, it's important to try to keep moving.

Read Carefully

Understand the problem. Read the question and answer choices carefully. Don't miss the question because you misread the terms. You have plenty of time to read each question thoroughly and make sure you understand what is being asked. Yet a happy medium must be attained, so don't waste too much time. You must read carefully, but efficiently.

Face Value

When in doubt, use common sense. Always accept the situation in the problem at face value. Don't read too much into it. These problems will not require you to make huge leaps of logic. The test writers aren't trying to throw you off with a cheap trick. If you have to go beyond creativity and make a leap of logic in order to have an answer choice answer the question, then you should look at the other answer choices. Don't overcomplicate the problem by creating theoretical relationships or explanations that will warp time or space. These are normal problems rooted in reality. It's just that the applicable relationship or explanation may not be readily apparent and you have to figure things out. Use your common sense to interpret anything that isn't clear.

Prefixes

If you're having trouble with a word in the question or answer choices, try dissecting it. Take advantage of every clue that the word might include. Prefixes and suffixes can be a huge help. Usually they allow you to determine a basic meaning. Pre- means before, post- means after, pro - is positive, de- is negative. From these prefixes and suffixes, you can get an idea of the general meaning of the word and try to put it into context. Beware though of any traps. Just because con is the opposite of pro, doesn't necessarily mean congress is the opposite of progress!

Hedge Phrases

Watch out for critical "hedge" phrases, such as likely, may, can, will often, sometimes, often, almost, mostly, usually, generally, rarely, sometimes. Question writers insert these hedge phrases to cover every possibility. Often an answer choice will be wrong simply because it leaves no room for exception. Avoid answer choices that have definitive words like "exactly," and "always".

Switchback Words

Stay alert for "switchbacks". These are the words and phrases frequently used to alert you to shifts in thought. The most common switchback word is "but". Others include although, however, nevertheless, on the other hand, even though, while, in spite of, despite, regardless of.

New Information

Correct answer choices will rarely have completely new information included. Answer choices typically are straightforward reflections of the material asked about and will directly relate to the question. If a new piece of information is included in an answer choice that doesn't even seem to relate to the topic being asked about, then that answer choice is likely incorrect. All of the information needed to answer the question is usually provided for you, and so you should not have to make guesses that are unsupported or choose answer choices that require unknown information that cannot be reasoned on its own.

Time Management

On technical questions, don't get lost on the technical terms. Don't spend too much time on any one question. If you don't know what a term means, then since you don't have a dictionary, odds are you aren't going to get much further. You should immediately recognize terms as whether or not you know them. If you don't, work with the other clues that you have, the other answer choices and terms provided, but don't waste too much time trying to figure out a difficult term.

Contextual Clues

Look for contextual clues. An answer can be right but not correct. The contextual clues will help you find the answer that is most right and is correct. Understand the context in which a phrase or statement is made. This will help you make important distinctions.

Don't Panic

Panicking will not answer any questions for you. Therefore, it isn't helpful. When you first see the question, if your mind goes blank, take a deep breath. Force yourself to mechanically go through the steps of solving the problem and using the strategies you've learned.

Pace Yourself

Don't get clock fever. It's easy to be overwhelmed when you're looking at a page full of questions, your mind is full of random thoughts and feeling confused, and the clock is ticking down faster than you would like. Calm down and maintain the pace that you have set for yourself. As long as you are on track by monitoring your pace, you are guaranteed to have enough time for yourself. When you get to the last few minutes of the test, it may seem like you won't have enough time left, but if you only have as many questions as you should have left at that point, then you're right on track!

Answer Selection

The best way to pick an answer choice is to eliminate all of those that are wrong, until only one is left and confirm that is the correct answer. Sometimes though, an answer choice may immediately look right. Be careful! Take a second to make sure that the other choices are not equally obvious. Don't make a hasty mistake. There are only two times that you should stop before checking other answers. First is when you are positive that the answer choice you have selected is correct. Second is when time is almost out and you have to make a quick guess!

Check Your Work

Since you will probably not know every term listed and the answer to every question, it is important that you get credit for the ones that you do know. Don't miss any questions through careless mistakes. If at all possible, try to take a second to look back over your answer selection and make sure you've selected the correct answer choice and haven't made a costly careless mistake (such as marking an answer choice that you didn't mean to mark). This quick double check should more than pay for itself in caught mistakes for the time it costs.

Beware of Directly Quoted Answers

Sometimes an answer choice will repeat word for word a portion of the question or reference section. However, beware of such exact duplication – it may be a trap! More than likely, the correct choice will paraphrase or summarize a point, rather than being exactly the same wording.

Slang

Scientific sounding answers are better than slang ones. An answer choice that begins "To compare the outcomes..." is much more likely to be correct than one that begins "Because some people insisted..."

Extreme Statements

Avoid wild answers that throw out highly controversial ideas that are proclaimed as established fact. An answer choice that states the "process should be used in certain situations, if..." is much more likely to be correct than one that states the "process should be discontinued completely." The first is a calm rational statement and doesn't even make a definitive, uncompromising stance, using a hedge word "if" to provide wiggle room, whereas the second choice is a radical idea and far more extreme.

Answer Choice Families

When you have two or more answer choices that are direct opposites or parallels, one of them is usually the correct answer. For instance, if one answer choice states "x increases" and another answer choice states "x decreases" or "y increases," then those two or three answer choices are very similar in construction and fall into the same family of answer choices. A family of answer choices is when two or three answer choices are very similar in construction, and yet often have a directly opposite meaning. Usually the correct answer choice will be in that family of answer choices. The "odd man out" or answer choice that doesn't seem to fit the parallel construction of the other answer choices is more likely to be incorrect.

How to Overcome Test Anxiety

The very nature of tests caters to some level of anxiety, nervousness or tension, just as we feel for any important event that occurs in our lives. A little bit of anxiety or nervousness can be a good thing. It helps us with motivation, and makes achievement just that much sweeter. However, too much anxiety can be a problem; especially if it hinders our ability to function and perform.

"Test anxiety," is the term that refers to the emotional reactions that some test-takers experience when faced with a test or exam. Having a fear of testing and exams is based upon a rational fear, since the test-taker's performance can shape the course of an academic career. Nevertheless, experiencing excessive fear of examinations will only interfere with the test-takers ability to perform, and his/her chances to be successful.

There are a large variety of causes that can contribute to the development and sensation of test anxiety. These include, but are not limited to lack of performance and worrying about issues surrounding the test.

Lack of Preparation

Lack of preparation can be identified by the following behaviors or situations:

Not scheduling enough time to study, and therefore cramming the night before the test or exam
Managing time poorly, to create the sensation that there is not enough time to do everything
Failing to organize the text information in advance, so that the study material consists of the entire text and not simply the pertinent information
Poor overall studying habits

Worrying, on the other hand, can be related to both the test taker, or many other factors around him/her that will be affected by the results of the test. These include worrying about:

Previous performances on similar exams, or exams in general
How friends and other students are achieving
The negative consequences that will result from a poor grade or failure

There are three primary elements to test anxiety. Physical components, which involve the same typical bodily reactions as those to acute anxiety (to be discussed below). Emotional factors have to do with fear or panic. Mental or cognitive issues concerning attention spans and memory abilities.

Physical Signals

There are many different symptoms of test anxiety, and these are not limited to mental and emotional strain. Frequently there are a range of physical signals that will let a test taker know that he/she is suffering from test anxiety. These bodily changes can include the following:

Perspiring
Sweaty palms
Wet, trembling hands
Nausea
Dry mouth
A knot in the stomach
Headache
Faintness
Muscle tension
Aching shoulders, back and neck
Rapid heart beat
Feeling too hot/cold

To recognize the sensation of test anxiety, a test-taker should monitor him/herself for the following sensations:

The physical distress symptoms as listed above
Emotional sensitivity, expressing emotional feelings such as the need to cry or laugh too much, or a sensation of anger or helplessness
A decreased ability to think, causing the test-taker to blank out or have racing thoughts that are hard to organize or control.

Though most students will feel some level of anxiety when faced with a test or exam, the majority can cope with that anxiety and maintain it at a manageable level. However, those who cannot are faced with a very real and very serious condition, which can and should be controlled for the immeasurable benefit of this sufferer.

Naturally, these sensations lead to negative results for the testing experience. The most common effects of test anxiety have to do with nervousness and mental blocking.

Nervousness

Nervousness can appear in several different levels:

The test-taker's difficulty, or even inability to read and understand the questions on the test
The difficulty or inability to organize thoughts to a coherent form
The difficulty or inability to recall key words and concepts relating to the testing questions (especially essays)
The receipt of poor grades on a test, though the test material was well known by the test taker

Conversely, a person may also experience mental blocking, which involves:

Blanking out on test questions
Only remembering the correct answers to the questions when the test has already finished.

Fortunately for test anxiety sufferers, beating these feelings, to a large degree, has to do with proper preparation. When a test taker has a feeling of preparedness, then anxiety will be dramatically lessened.

The first step to resolving anxiety issues is to distinguish which of the two types of anxiety are being suffered. If the anxiety is a direct result of a lack of preparation, this should be considered a normal reaction, and the anxiety level (as opposed to the test results) shouldn't be anything to worry about. However, if, when adequately prepared, the test-taker still panics, blanks out, or seems to overreact, this is not a fully rational reaction. While this can be considered normal too, there are many ways to combat and overcome these effects.

Remember that anxiety cannot be entirely eliminated, however, there are ways to minimize it, to make the anxiety easier to manage. Preparation is one of the best ways to minimize test anxiety. Therefore the following techniques are wise in order to best fight off any anxiety that may want to build.

To begin with, try to avoid cramming before a test, whenever it is possible. By trying to memorize an entire term's worth of information in one day, you'll be shocking your system, and not giving yourself a very good chance to absorb the information. This is an easy path to anxiety, so for those who suffer from test anxiety, cramming should not even be considered an option.

Instead of cramming, work throughout the semester to combine all of the material which is presented throughout the semester, and work on it gradually as the course goes by, making sure to master the main concepts first, leaving minor details for a week or so before the test.

To study for the upcoming exam, be sure to pose questions that may be on the examination, to gauge the ability to answer them by integrating the ideas from your texts, notes and lectures, as well as any supplementary readings.

If it is truly impossible to cover all of the information that was covered in that particular term, concentrate on the most important portions, that can be covered very well. Learn these concepts as best as possible, so that when the test comes, a goal can be made to use these concepts as presentations of your knowledge.

In addition to study habits, changes in attitude are critical to beating a struggle with test anxiety. In fact, an improvement of the perspective over the entire test-taking experience can actually help a test taker to enjoy studying and therefore improve the overall experience. Be certain not to overemphasize the significance of the grade - know that the result of the test is neither a reflection of self worth, nor is it a measure of intelligence; one grade will not predict a person's future success.

To improve an overall testing outlook, the following steps should be tried:

Keeping in mind that the most reasonable expectation for taking a test is to expect to try to demonstrate as much of what you know as you possibly can.
Reminding ourselves that a test is only one test; this is not the only one, and there will be others.
The thought of thinking of oneself in an irrational, all-or-nothing term should be avoided at all costs.
A reward should be designated for after the test, so there's something to look forward to. Whether it be going to a movie, going out to eat, or simply visiting friends, schedule it in advance, and do it no matter what result is expected on the exam.

Test-takers should also keep in mind that the basics are some of the most important things, even beyond anti-anxiety techniques and studying. Never neglect the basic social, emotional and biological needs, in order to try to absorb information. In order to best achieve, these three factors must be held as just as important as the studying itself.

Study Steps

Remember the following important steps for studying:

Maintain healthy nutrition and exercise habits. Continue both your recreational activities and social pass times. These both contribute to your physical and emotional well being.
Be certain to get a good amount of sleep, especially the night before the test, because when you're overtired you are not able to perform to the best of your best ability.
Keep the studying pace to a moderate level by taking breaks when they are needed, and varying the work whenever possible, to keep the mind fresh instead of getting bored. When enough studying has been done that all the material that can be learned has been learned, and the test taker is prepared for the test, stop studying and do something relaxing such as listening to music, watching a movie, or taking a warm bubble bath.

There are also many other techniques to minimize the uneasiness or apprehension that is experienced along with test anxiety before, during, or even after the examination. In fact, there are a great deal of things that can be done to stop anxiety from interfering with lifestyle and performance. Again, remember that anxiety will not be eliminated entirely, and it shouldn't be. Otherwise that "up" feeling for exams would not exist, and most of us depend on that sensation to perform better than usual. However, this anxiety has to be at a level that is manageable.

Of course, as we have just discussed, being prepared for the exam is half the battle right away. Attending all classes, finding out what knowledge will be expected on the exam, and knowing the exam schedules are easy steps to lowering anxiety. Keeping up with work will remove the need to cram, and efficient study habits will eliminate wasted time. Studying should be done in an ideal location for concentration, so that it is simple to become interested in the material and give it complete attention. A method such as SQ3R (Survey, Question, Read, Recite, Review) is a wonderful key to follow to make sure that the study habits are as effective as possible, especially in the case of learning from a textbook. Flashcards are great techniques for memorization. Learning to take good

- 69 -

notes will mean that notes will be full of useful information, so that less sifting will need to be done to seek out what is pertinent for studying. Reviewing notes after class and then again on occasion will keep the information fresh in the mind. From notes that have been taken summary sheets and outlines can be made for simpler reviewing.

A study group can also be a very motivational and helpful place to study, as there will be a sharing of ideas, all of the minds can work together, to make sure that everyone understands, and the studying will be made more interesting because it will be a social occasion.

Basically, though, as long as the test-taker remains organized and self confident, with efficient study habits, less time will need to be spent studying, and higher grades will be achieved.

To become self confident, there are many useful steps. The first of these is "self talk." It has been shown through extensive research, that self-talk for students who suffer from test anxiety, should be well monitored, in order to make sure that it contributes to self confidence as opposed to sinking the student. Frequently the self talk of test-anxious students is negative or self-defeating, thinking that everyone else is smarter and faster, that they always mess up, and that if they don't do well, they'll fail the entire course. It is important to decreasing anxiety that awareness is made of self talk. Try writing any negative self thoughts and then disputing them with a positive statement instead. Begin self-encouragement as though it was a friend speaking. Repeat positive statements to help reprogram the mind to believing in successes instead of failures.

Helpful Techniques

Other extremely helpful techniques include:

Self-visualization of doing well and reaching goals
While aiming for an "A" level of understanding, don't try to "overprotect" by setting your expectations lower. This will only convince the mind to stop studying in order to meet the lower expectations.
Don't make comparisons with the results or habits of other students. These are individual factors, and different things work for different people, causing different results.
Strive to become an expert in learning what works well, and what can be done in order to improve. Consider collecting this data in a journal.
Create rewards for after studying instead of doing things before studying that will only turn into avoidance behaviors.
Make a practice of relaxing - by using methods such as progressive relaxation, self-hypnosis, guided imagery, etc - in order to make relaxation an automatic sensation.
Work on creating a state of relaxed concentration so that concentrating will take on the focus of the mind, so that none will be wasted on worrying.
Take good care of the physical self by eating well and getting enough sleep.
Plan in time for exercise and stick to this plan.

Beyond these techniques, there are other methods to be used before, during and after the test that will help the test-taker perform well in addition to overcoming anxiety.

Before the exam comes the academic preparation. This involves establishing a study schedule and beginning at least one week before the actual date of the test. By doing this, the anxiety of not having enough time to study for the test will be automatically eliminated. Moreover, this will make the studying a much more effective experience, ensuring that the learning will be an easier process. This relieves much undue pressure on the test-taker.

Summary sheets, note cards, and flash cards with the main concepts and examples of these main concepts should be prepared in advance of the actual studying time. A topic should never be eliminated from this process. By omitting a topic because it isn't expected to be on the test is only setting up the test-taker for anxiety should it actually appear on the exam. Utilize the course syllabus for laying out the topics that should be studied. Carefully go over the notes that were made in class, paying special attention to any of the issues that the professor took special care to emphasize while lecturing in class. In the textbooks, use the chapter review, or if possible, the chapter tests, to begin your review.

It may even be possible to ask the instructor what information will be covered on the exam, or what the format of the exam will be (for example, multiple choice, essay, free form, true-false). Additionally, see if it is possible to find out how many questions will be on the test. If a review sheet or sample test has been offered by the professor, make good use of it, above anything else, for the preparation for the test. Another great resource for getting to know the examination is reviewing tests from previous semesters. Use these tests to review, and aim to achieve a 100% score on each of the possible topics. With a few exceptions, the goal that you set for yourself is the highest one that you will reach.

Take all of the questions that were assigned as homework, and rework them to any other possible course material. The more problems reworked, the more skill and confidence will form as a result. When forming the solution to a problem, write out each of the steps. Don't simply do head work. By doing as many steps on paper as possible, much clarification and therefore confidence will be formed. Do this with as many homework problems as possible, before checking the answers. By checking the answer after each problem, a reinforcement will exist, that will not be on the exam. Study situations should be as exam-like as possible, to prime the test-taker's system for the experience. By waiting to check the answers at the end, a psychological advantage will be formed, to decrease the stress factor.

Another fantastic reason for not cramming is the avoidance of confusion in concepts, especially when it comes to mathematics. 8-10 hours of study will become one hundred percent more effective if it is spread out over a week or at least several days, instead of doing it all in one sitting. Recognize that the human brain requires time in order to assimilate new material, so frequent breaks and a span of study time over several days will be much more beneficial.

Additionally, don't study right up until the point of the exam. Studying should stop a minimum of one hour before the exam begins. This allows the brain to rest and put things in their proper order. This will also provide the time to become as relaxed as possible when going into the examination room. The test-taker will also have time to eat well and eat sensibly. Know that the brain needs food as much as the rest of the body. With enough food and enough sleep, as well as a relaxed attitude, the body and the mind are primed for success.

Avoid any anxious classmates who are talking about the exam. These students only spread anxiety, and are not worth sharing the anxious sentimentalities.

Before the test also involves creating a positive attitude, so mental preparation should also be a point of concentration. There are many keys to creating a positive attitude. Should fears become rushing in, make a visualization of taking the exam, doing well, and seeing an A written on the paper. Write out a list of affirmations that will bring a feeling of confidence, such as "I am doing well in my English class," "I studied well and know my material," "I enjoy this class." Even if the affirmations aren't believed at first, it sends a positive message to the subconscious which will result in an alteration of the overall belief system, which is the system that creates reality.

If a sensation of panic begins, work with the fear and imagine the very worst! Work through the entire scenario of not passing the test, failing the entire course, and dropping out of school, followed by not getting a job, and pushing a shopping cart through the dark alley where you'll live. This will place things into perspective! Then, practice deep breathing and create a visualization of the opposite situation - achieving an "A" on the exam, passing the entire course, receiving the degree at a graduation ceremony.

On the day of the test, there are many things to be done to ensure the best results, as well as the most calm outlook. The following stages are suggested in order to maximize test-taking potential:

Begin the examination day with a moderate breakfast, and avoid any coffee or beverages with caffeine if the test taker is prone to jitters. Even people who are used to managing caffeine can feel jittery or light-headed when it is taken on a test day.
Attempt to do something that is relaxing before the examination begins. As last minute cramming clouds the mastering of overall concepts, it is better to use this time to create a calming outlook.
Be certain to arrive at the test location well in advance, in order to provide time to select a location that is away from doors, windows and other distractions, as well as giving enough time to relax before the test begins.
Keep away from anxiety generating classmates who will upset the sensation of stability and relaxation that is being attempted before the exam.
Should the waiting period before the exam begins cause anxiety, create a self-distraction by reading a light magazine or something else that is relaxing and simple.

During the exam itself, read the entire exam from beginning to end, and find out how much time should be allotted to each individual problem. Once writing the exam, should more time be taken for a problem, it should be abandoned, in order to begin another problem. If there is time at the end, the unfinished problem can always be returned to and completed.

Read the instructions very carefully - twice - so that unpleasant surprises won't follow during or after the exam has ended.

When writing the exam, pretend that the situation is actually simply the completion of homework within a library, or at home. This will assist in forming a relaxed atmosphere, and will allow the brain extra focus for the complex thinking function.

Begin the exam with all of the questions with which the most confidence is felt. This will build the confidence level regarding the entire exam and will begin a quality momentum. This will also create encouragement for trying the problems where uncertainty resides.

Going with the "gut instinct" is always the way to go when solving a problem. Second guessing should be avoided at all costs. Have confidence in the ability to do well.

For essay questions, create an outline in advance that will keep the mind organized and make certain that all of the points are remembered. For multiple choice, read every answer, even if the correct one has been spotted - a better one may exist.

Continue at a pace that is reasonable and not rushed, in order to be able to work carefully. Provide enough time to go over the answers at the end, to check for small errors that can be corrected.

Should a feeling of panic begin, breathe deeply, and think of the feeling of the body releasing sand through its pores. Visualize a calm, peaceful place, and include all of the sights, sounds and sensations of this image. Continue the deep breathing, and take a few minutes to continue this with closed eyes. When all is well again, return to the test.

If a "blanking" occurs for a certain question, skip it and move on to the next question. There will be time to return to the other question later. Get everything done that can be done, first, to guarantee all the grades that can be compiled, and to build all of the confidence possible. Then return to the weaker questions to build the marks from there.

Remember, one's own reality can be created, so as long as the belief is there, success will follow. And remember: anxiety can happen later, right now, there's an exam to be written!

After the examination is complete, whether there is a feeling for a good grade or a bad grade, don't dwell on the exam, and be certain to follow through on the reward that was promised...and enjoy it! Don't dwell on any mistakes that have been made, as there is nothing that can be done at this point anyway.

Additionally, don't begin to study for the next test right away. Do something relaxing for a while, and let the mind relax and prepare itself to begin absorbing information again.

From the results of the exam - both the grade and the entire experience, be certain to learn from what has gone on. Perfect studying habits and work some more on confidence in order to make the next examination experience even better than the last one.

Learn to avoid places where openings occurred for laziness, procrastination and day dreaming.

Use the time between this exam and the next one to better learn to relax, even learning to relax on cue, so that any anxiety can be controlled during the next exam. Learn how to relax the body. Slouch in your chair if that helps. Tighten and then relax all of the different muscle groups, one group at a time, beginning with the feet and then working all the way up to the neck and face. This will ultimately relax the muscles more than they were to begin with. Learn how to breathe deeply and comfortably, and focus on this breathing going in and out as a relaxing thought. With every exhale, repeat the word "relax."

As common as test anxiety is, it is very possible to overcome it. Make yourself one of the test-takers who overcome this frustrating hindrance.

Additional Bonus Material

Due to our efforts to try to keep this book to a manageable length, we've created a link that will give you access to all of your additional bonus material.

Please visit http://www.mometrix.com/bonus948/staarg6read to access the information.